THE
FOLDING
BOOK

THE FOLDING BOOK

A COMPLETE GUIDE TO CREATING SPACE AND GETTING ORGANIZED

JANELLE COHEN

ROCK
POINT

Inspiring | Educating | Creating | Entertaining

Brimming with creative inspiration, how-to projects, and useful information to enrich your everyday life, quarto.com is a favorite destination for those pursuing their interests and passions.

Text © 2022 by Janelle Cohen
Photography © 2022 by Quarto Publishing Group USA Inc.

First published in 2022 by Rock Point,
an imprint of The Quarto Group,
142 West 36th Street, 4th Floor,
New York, NY 10018, USA
T (212) 779-4972 F (212) 779-6058
www.Quarto.com

Rock Point titles are also available at discount for retail, wholesale, promotional and bulk purchase. For details, contact the Special Sales Manager by email at specialsales@quarto.com or by mail at The Quarto Group, Attn: Special Sales Manager, 100 Cummings Center Suite, 265D, Beverly, MA 01915, USA.

10 9 8 7 6 5 4 3 2 1

ISBN: 978-1-63106-837-9

Library of Congress Control Number: 2021947618

Publisher: Rage Kindelsperger
Creative Director: Laura Drew
Managing Editor: Cara Donaldson
Senior Editor: Erin Canning
Cover and Interior Design: Evelin Kasikov
Photography: Mary Claire Roman

Printed in China

For Linda Levine and Sheri Goldner—
Two women who showed me how to
be bold, brave, and fearless.

Contents

Introduction **8**

Getting Started **10**

The Technique **12**

Folding Basics **14**

Editing While Folding **15**

Glossary **16**

Basics

18

Baby

100

Kid

152

Feminine

48

Masculine

88

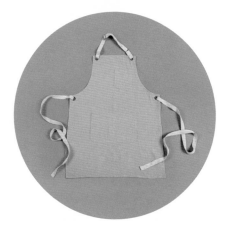

Linens

190

Travel

220

Index **232**

Acknowledgments **237**

About the Author **240**

Introduction

I have always been a detail-oriented and organized person, so much so that I turned these passions into my own business, Straighten Up by Janelle, which has grown into a personalized organization service, working with clients all over Los Angeles, including numerous celebrities and influencers. I believe that having an organized system in your home creates a more positive environment, and that it is possible to keep it maintained regardless of how busy life gets. Organizing your home doesn't have to be stressful and can even be easy and enjoyable. Yes, you read that correctly—enjoyable!

Though I organize all aspects of my clients' homes, in this book, I focus on one of the simplest, quickest, and inexpensive ways to create space, get organized, and save time: folding. That's right! When your clothes and linens are folded compactly, with everything visible in drawers and baskets or on shelves, you spend less time sorting through piles each day and can continually weed out things that are no longer useful to you and your family.

I also find folding to be therapeutic. We live in a chaotic world filled with a lot of unpredictability, and folding (and organizing in general) allows you to be present and in control, even if just for a few minutes. When I feel anxious or stressed, I fold. If you are thinking to yourself, "What's with this chick?" just give folding a chance. I promise, once you hone your folding technique, it will become the easiest and most enjoyable chore you have. I recently found a video of myself at two years old folding to perfection with an iron and everything!

My parents don't remember me loving to fold as a kid, and honestly neither do I. But when I watch that video, I feel like folding has been inside me forever. I would definitely hire two-year-old me as my assistant. That's how much I nailed it! With that said, if baby Janelle can do it, so can you.

Folding is one of those things that you have probably done forever, or at least since you started doing your own laundry. But . . . did you ever really learn how to properly do it? Maybe you learned while working retail with a piece of cardboard. Whether you aspire to fold like a pro or you never knew this is what you needed in your life, I'm here to show you how to do it. After many years as a professional organizer, I have figured out what really works—not just what visually looks the prettiest and is Instagram-worthy, but what is realistic. My method is easy to master with a little bit of practice and easy to apply in everyday life.

You can follow my folding technique exactly or use it as a jumping-off point for your own technique, because there is no wrong way to fold. The right way is what works for you, your family, and your lifestyle. Pick and choose what feels like a good fit and set realistic goals that you can surpass (rather than out-of-reach goals that may stress you out). If you are someone who isn't going to fold your underwear, then don't. Live your life! My goal with this book is to help you establish an organization system that you can maintain and even enjoy doing.

Happy folding!

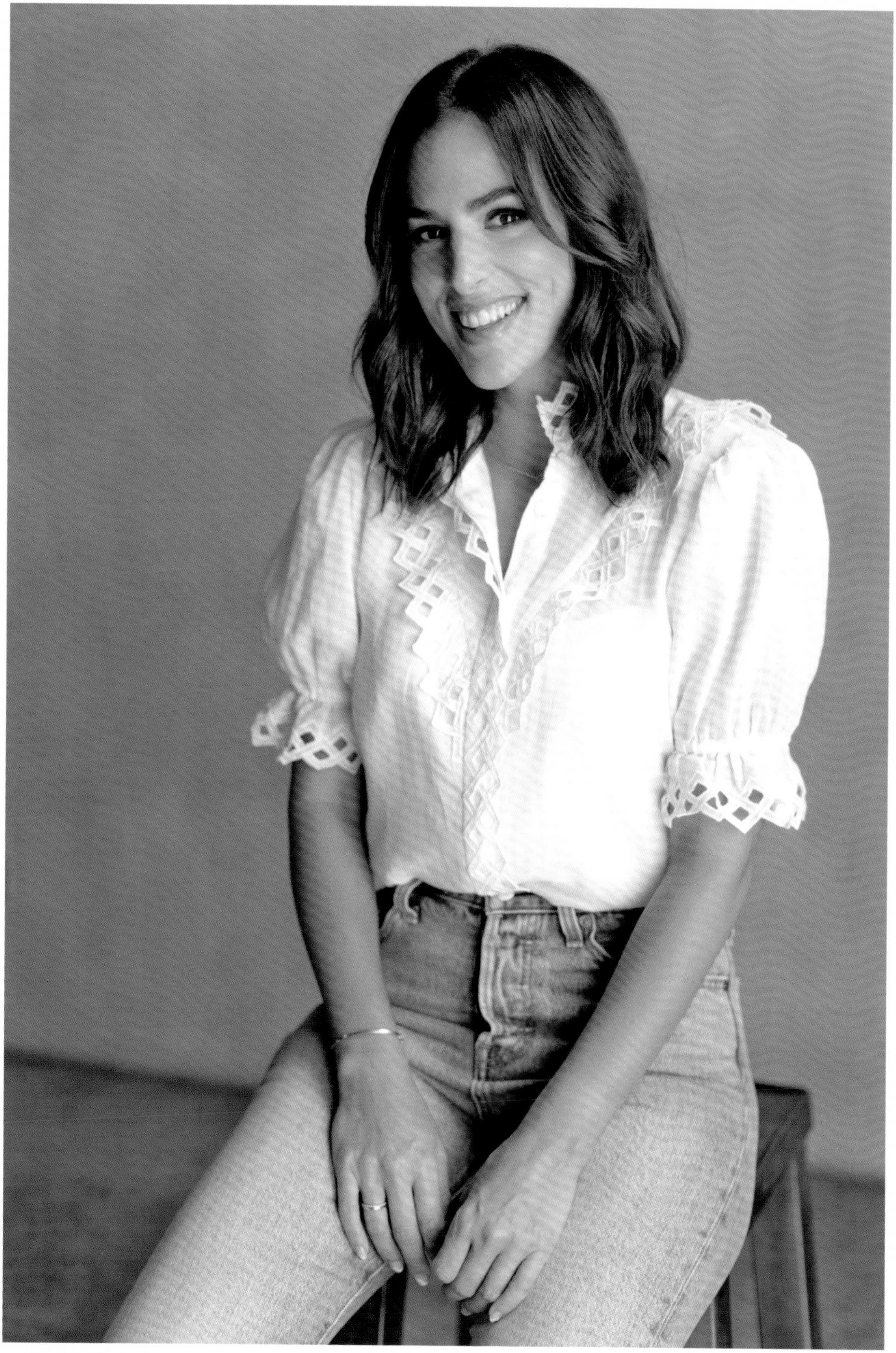

Getting Started

You already have everything you need to start folding. You can start with that basket of clean laundry fresh out of the dryer, you can leisurely organize one drawer at a time, or you can dump out all your drawers and refold everything at once. It's up to you! Again, the purpose of this book isn't to make you feel stressed out or overwhelmed about folding and having everything look perfect. Working at your own pace will make it feel like less of a chore and more of a fun project. You also don't need to invest in more storage. Work with what you already own, whether that be dressers, shelves, or baskets. Once you get further into folding and organizing, you can assess what else may best suit your needs. Here's how to get started.

Folding vs. Hanging

Most articles of clothing can be folded for a drawer, basket, or shelf, but some things should always be hung. Here's what you need to know.

Things you should always hang: blouses, dresses, blazers, dress pants, bulky jackets, coats

Things you should always fold: undergarments, socks, tank tops, sweaters, leggings, sweatpants, pajamas, workout clothes, swimwear, linens

Things that can be folded or hung: T-shirts, button-downs, polo shirts, sweatshirts, casual pants, denim, skirts (depending on the fabric), nightgowns (depending on the fabric)

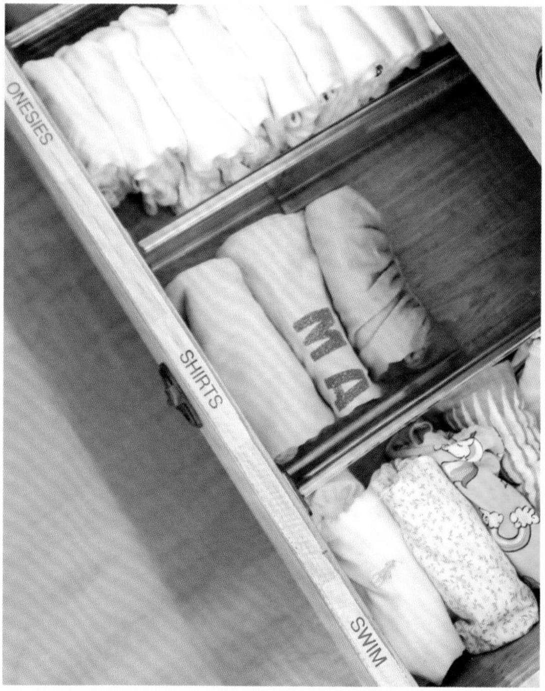
ONESIES
SHIRTS
SWIM

Organizing Dressers

I like to organize dressers from head to toe and short to long. In the top drawer, I place undergarments, layering tank tops, and socks. I then move down to tops (tanks, short sleeves, and then long sleeves), followed by bottoms (shorts/skirts, capris, long pants, and sweatpants). And at the very bottom, I place pajamas and specialty items (swimwear, shapewear, etc.).

If I am organizing a kid's room, I label each drawer/row of clothing so that everyone in the home knows what is where, and the child can have ownership over their space. Adding little graphics can help with kids who can't read yet. It can't hurt to start organization young so that it becomes second nature.

How to Label a Kid's Dresser

Folding children's clothing can be slightly more confusing than adult clothes. This is because adults know their inventory, so they can easily open a drawer and pull out what they need. Many people tend to take care of children, so it needs to be identifiable to everyone without any explanation. Here's an easy way to label a kid's drawers to know what's where and evolve with them.

1. Organize by item category (onesies, shirts, pants, pajamas, etc.). Each category should have its own row in a drawer. Typically, categories share a drawer because baby and children's clothes are so small.

2. Add a label for each category to the lip of the drawer, lined up with each row. If you don't have a label maker, cut a thin piece of masking or painter's tape and write on it with a Sharpie. It doesn't need to be fancy to be practical.

3. For a baby, label the top middle of the drawer with the size (0–3 months, 3–6 months, 6–9 months, etc.). When the child ages up, you just need to rip off/replace the size label. The rows can stay the same, just with the next size up. Once this system is in place, it is easy to maintain and adjust as the child continues to grow.

The Technique

The folding technique used throughout this book is called "file folding." File folding is basically filing your clothes in a drawer (or basket) like you would file paperwork. It's annoying to search through a stack of papers rather than flip through a file cabinet, and the same thing goes for clothing.

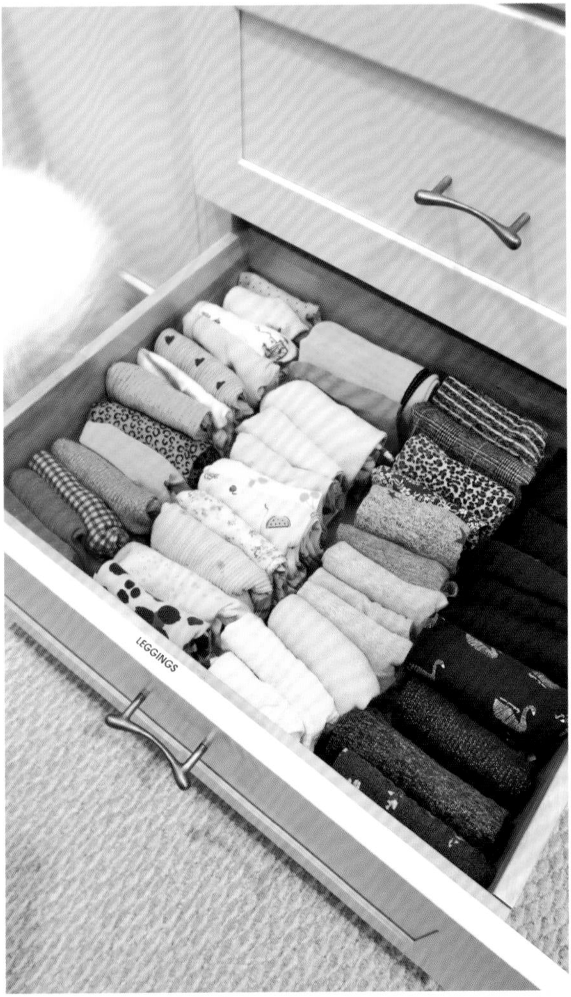
LEGGINGS

With file folding, each drawer or row is a different category of clothing, and nothing gets lost at the bottom of a pile of clothes. If you stack your clothes in a drawer, you will be continuously picking what is on top because it is easiest to grab. Or if you know something is at the bottom, then you have to mess up the pile and dig through to find what you're looking for. So, rather than having, say, a big stack of T-shirts to sort through, you have a visual of every T-shirt right off the bat. There are many benefits to file folding, with the main ones being that it is incredibly space saving and increases visibility.

Keep in mind that file folding is something that takes practice and you aren't going to fold every piece perfect right off the bat. So don't give up or get frustrated when you open your drawers and they don't look Instagram-worthy. Find what works for you and you will benefit from your unique organization system.

A file-folded item has a rounded edge and an open edge. The open edge acts like legs (see page 16) to help the folded item stand in a drawer or basket.

Here are some examples of file-folded items from a top view and a side view so that you can see how the items look when folded.

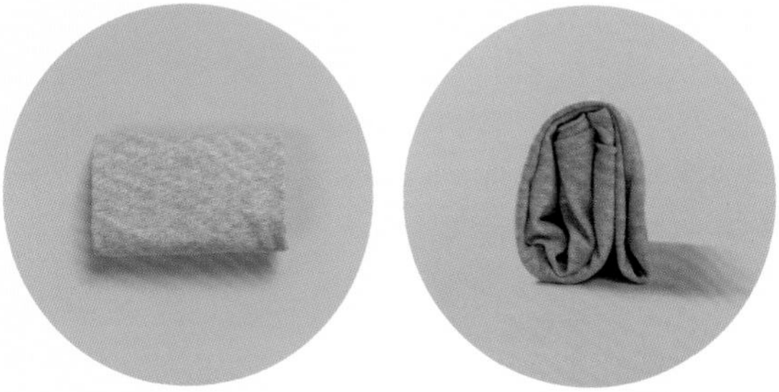

Adult Tank Top

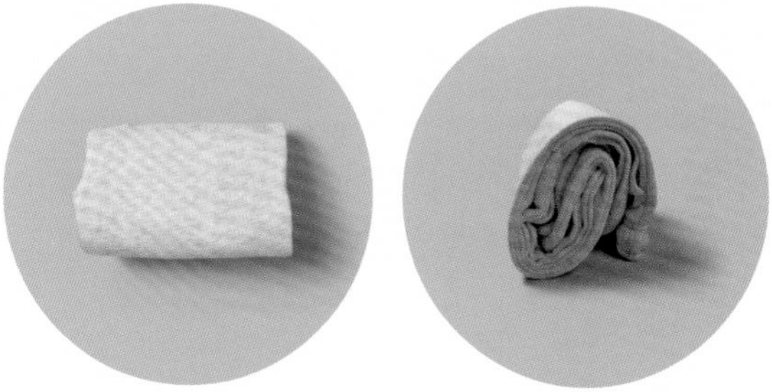

Adult Sweatpants

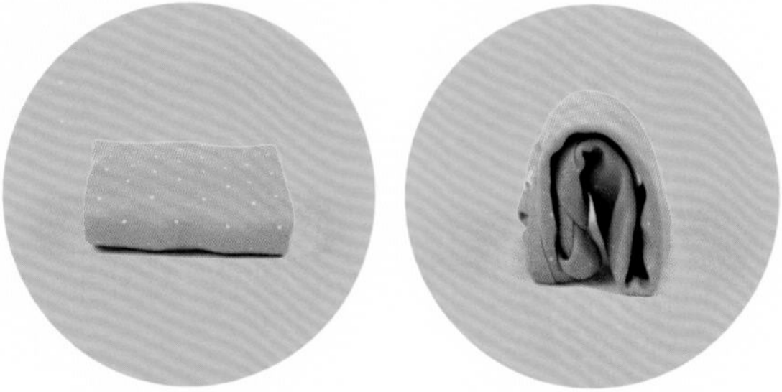

Baby Onesie

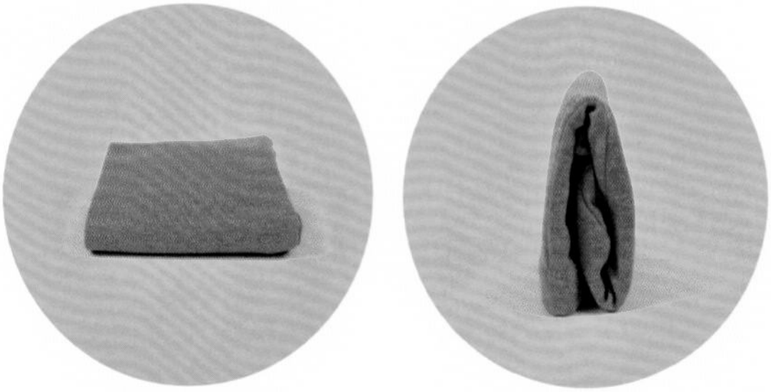

Baby Leggings

Folding Basics

Here are some general tips to keep in mind while you are folding.

- Always fold on a flat surface, such as a dining table, desk, bed, or ironing board. It's easier to not have to bend over.

- Smooth out any wrinkles with your hands before you start folding. I find an iron to be a little extra, especially if you are trying to maintain this organization method.

- Keep your lines smooth/flat (again, using your hands to smooth out any wrinkles) while you are folding. The smoother the clothes are, the less bulky the folds will be. This is also the key to helping your rows look clean and consistent.

- Always close buttons, snaps, and zippers to make folding easier.

- As you will see throughout the book, I usually fold from right to left, because that feels natural to me, but you can fold from left to right. Just be consistent with the direction you choose.

- Keep rows modular by folding shirts, pants, and the like the same width even when they are different styles and sizes. Sometimes you have to "cheat" a little to fold your items to the same size. Fold in a narrow tee less than a looser-fitting one. Fold over the booty triangle (see page 16) a little farther on a larger pair of pants. Fold up a longer garment an extra time. Choose a folded item in each category as a guide for how wide you want all the folds in that category to be so that the rows in the drawer line up perfectly. The more modular, the more you will maximize space.

- Always fold children's clothing so that you can easily see the neckline. Then you can quickly see the size and don't need to unfold the whole item to make sure you have the correct one. Kids (especially babies) grow quickly, so you want to be able to easily peek through their drawers to pull out what they have outgrown.

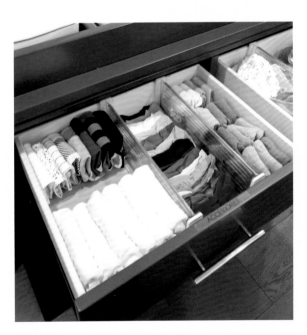

Editing While Folding

No time is more perfect for deciding what to keep and what isn't serving you anymore than while you are folding and organizing. Not only can you weed out things like outgrown children's clothing and undergarments and socks that have seen better days, but also those items that seem to hang around but are never worn. Here are some questions I like to ask my clients when helping them organize their drawers and closets.

1. **Does it fit you?** If your weight has fluctuated, would you be able to purchase the item again or is it irreplaceable? If you can replace it, so long.

2. **Is it damaged?** Would you pay to get it fixed or take the time to fix it yourself? If not, say good-bye.

3. **Does it make you feel good when you wear it?** If the answer is no, see you later. It is not even worth downgrading something that doesn't make you feel good to the clothes that you only wear around the house. You should feel incredible 100 percent of the time.

4. **Would you wear it tomorrow (if it was the right occasion)?** No? Get rid of it. If you bought a dress for a wedding, let's say, and are still not going to wear it, why are you saving it for a hypothetical situation? The same goes with keeping something for a potential costume that you would only wear once anyway. I would suggest keeping an accessory for a costume but not an entire outfit. (You would be surprised by how creative you can get using pieces you already have in your closet.)

5. **Would you want to be seen wearing it in photos?** If not, then good riddance. These days, your photo can be taken at any time, so think about if you would want an item of clothing to be immortalized in a photo. You will want to look back on a photo twenty years later and think, "I really liked that shirt," even if it has gone out of fashion.

6. **Can it be worn with more than one outfit?** If not, see ya. Something to consider for future purchases is cost per wear (see page 16), and the cost per wear is going to be high for a specific thing bought to wear with another specific thing. Another variable to consider when shopping for clothes is the care instructions for the item. If having to take an item to the dry cleaner is going add stress to your life, then look for things that you can include in the wash, or vice versa.

7. **Are you keeping it for sentimental reasons?** This is probably the most difficult decision to make when getting rid of clothes. If you still want to keep it, store it in an area for sentimental keepsakes and not in your closet (but you'll still want to be selective with what you store here). You want your wardrobe to be an active item in your life, not cluttered with things you're never going to wear again.

As you maintain this organization system over time, continue editing. Sometimes the hardest part about getting rid of things is forcing yourself to do it in one go, which can be overwhelming. If you find yourself having a hard time, the good news is that a friend or family member may love the item or you can consider donation or resale.

Glossary

These are words and phrases that you will continually come across throughout the book, so here's a quick guide with their meanings.

Booty Triangle

This is the extra flap of fabric that forms/sticks out when you fold any bottoms in half. It resembles a little triangle and is located at the butt, or the booty (as I like to call it).

Cost Per Wear

This is the cost of an item of clothing divided by the number of times you wear it. If you invest in a coat that costs $200 and you only wear it ten times, it has a high cost per wear—$20 per wear. If you invest in jeans that also cost $200 and you wear them twice a week for a year, it has a low cost per wear—$1.92 per wear.

Facedown

This is when the front side of an item of clothing is lying down on the folding surface.

Faceup

This is when the back side of an item of clothing is lying down on the folding surface.

Fold in Half

This is when you fold one half of a clothing item over the other half and align the two sides, either horizontally (right to left, left to right) or vertically (bottom to top, top to bottom).

Fold in Thirds

This is when you fold up the bottom edge of a clothing item to the middle and then fold up the bottom again and align it with the top, creating legs (see below) for the item to stand on when filed in a drawer.

Grab and Go

This refers to folded sets of items—pajamas, sweat suits, swimsuits, bedding—that can be quickly grabbed by adults and children alike to make life a little easier and save time.

Legs

When an item is file-folded, it has a smooth, rounded edge (see below) and an open side with flaps that act as legs to help the folded item stand in a drawer.

Overcrossing

You want your edges to align when folding and avoid having one edge cross over another.

Rounded Edge

When you file-fold, you always want this side of the fold facing up. The opposite, open, side acts like legs (see above) and keeps the folded item standing upright in the drawer. When folding an item for a shelf, you want the rounded edge facing out.

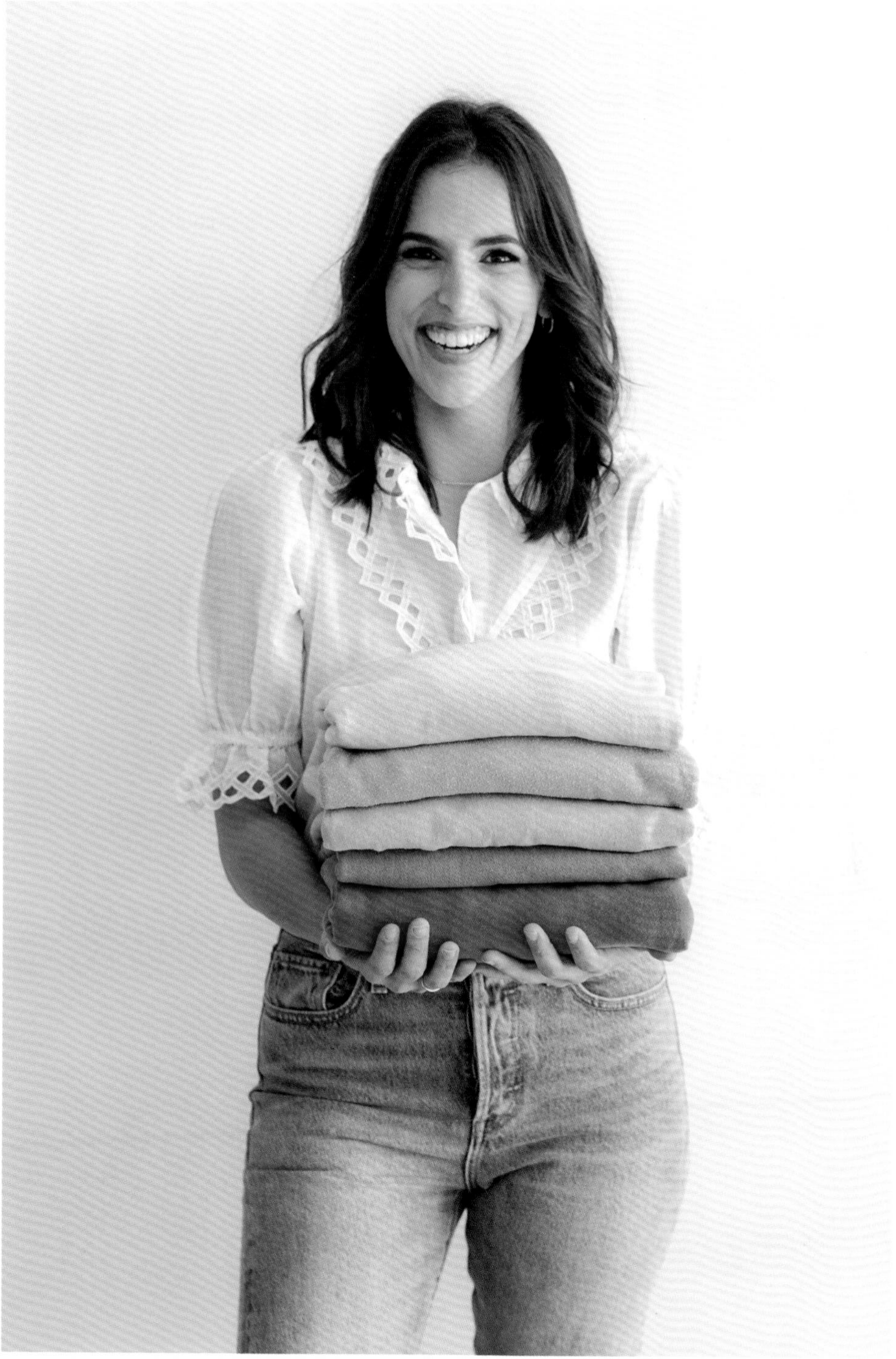

Basics

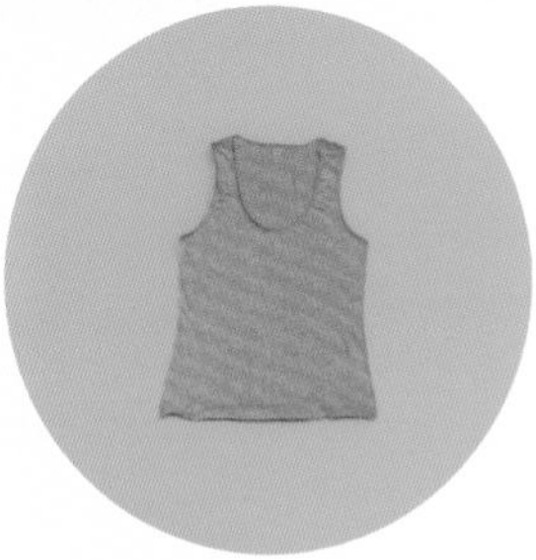

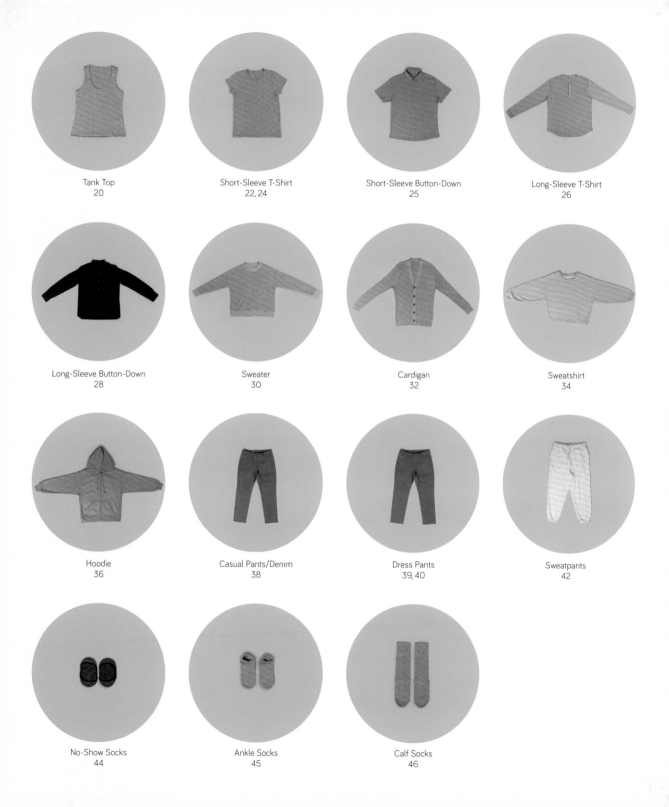

Tank Top
20

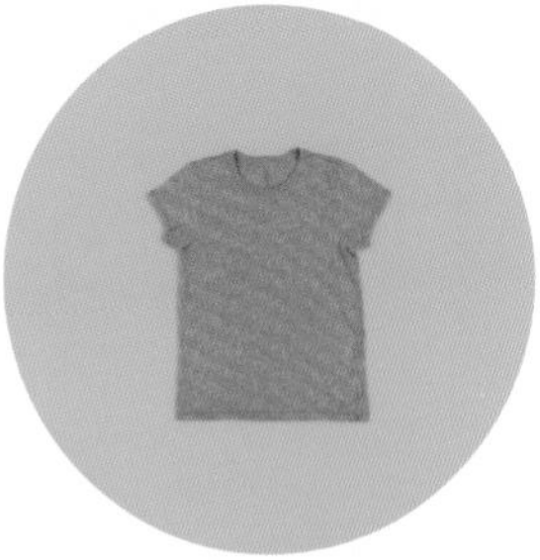

Short-Sleeve T-Shirt
22, 24

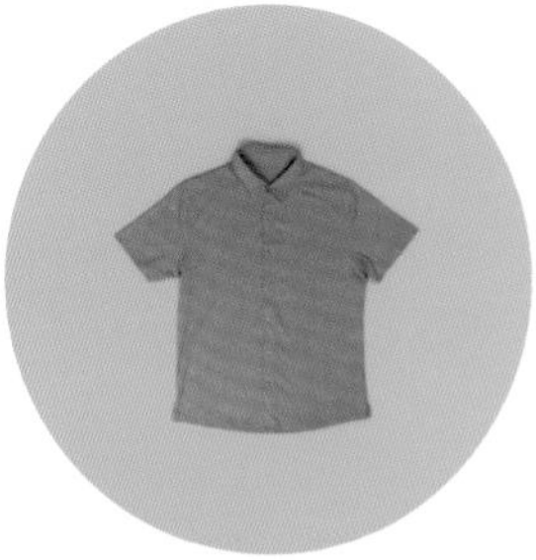

Short-Sleeve Button-Down
25

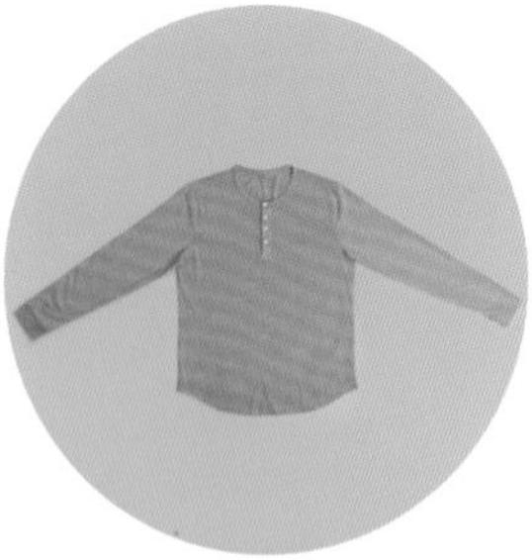

Long-Sleeve T-Shirt
26

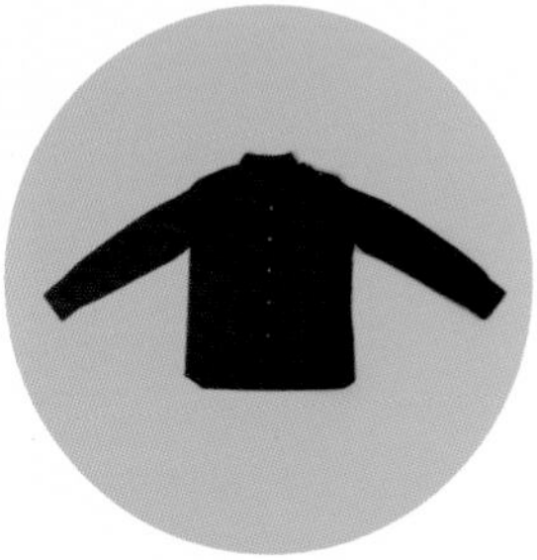

Long-Sleeve Button-Down
28

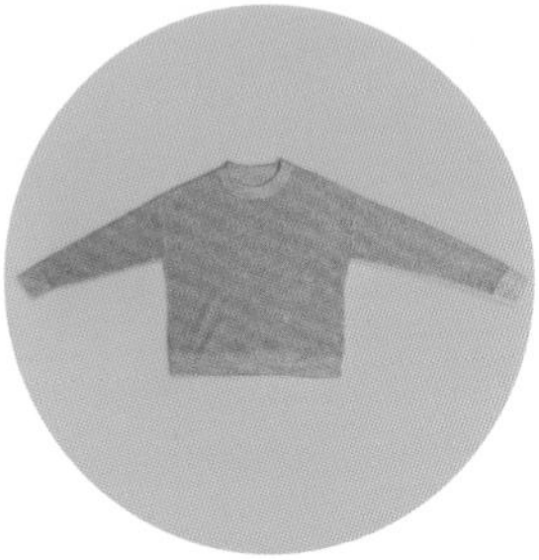

Sweater
30

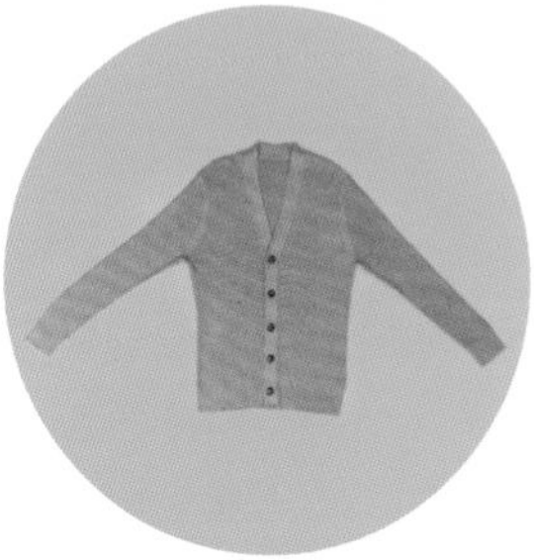

Cardigan
32

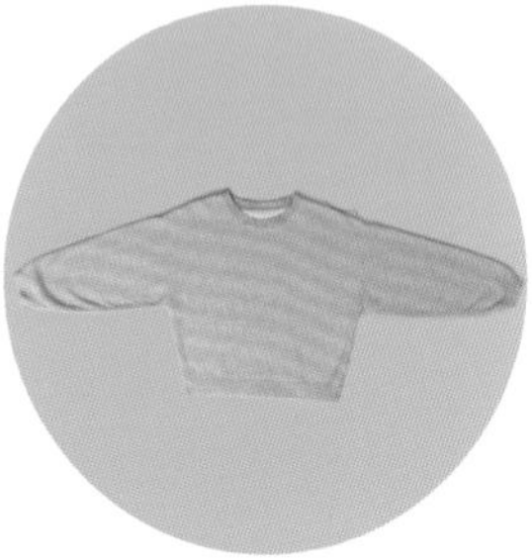

Sweatshirt
34

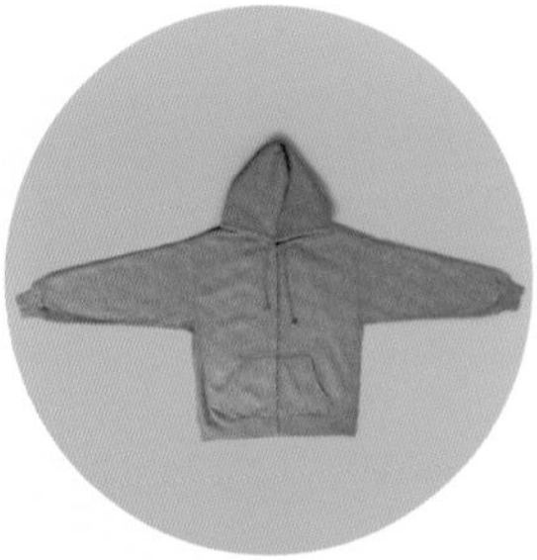

Hoodie
36

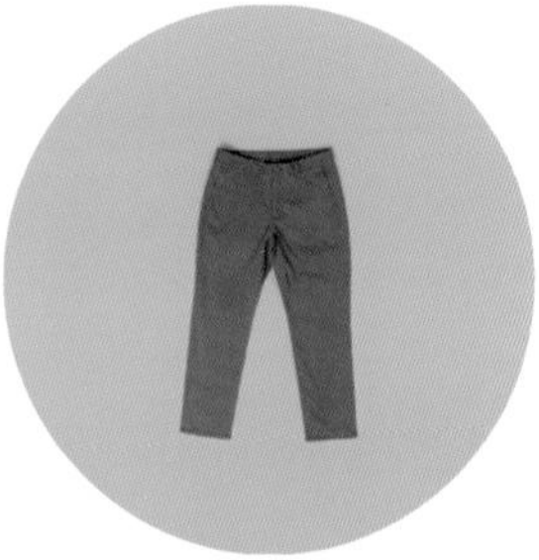

Casual Pants/Denim
38

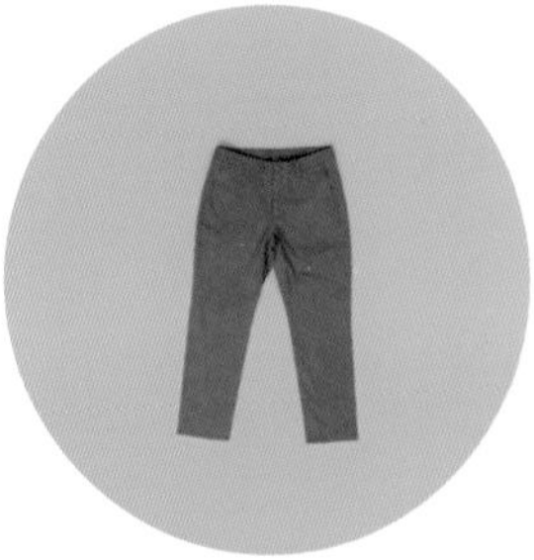

Dress Pants
39, 40

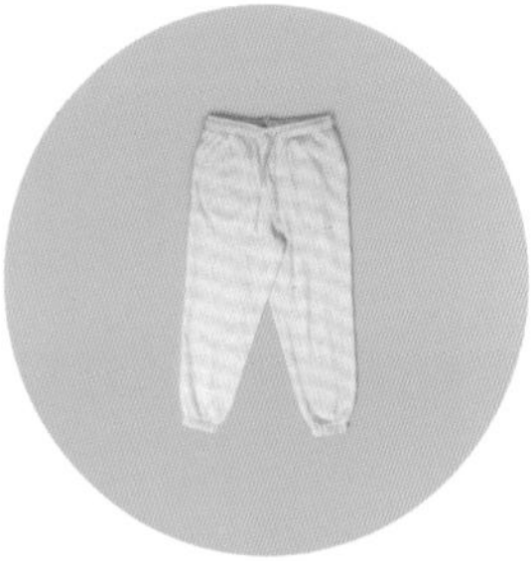

Sweatpants
42

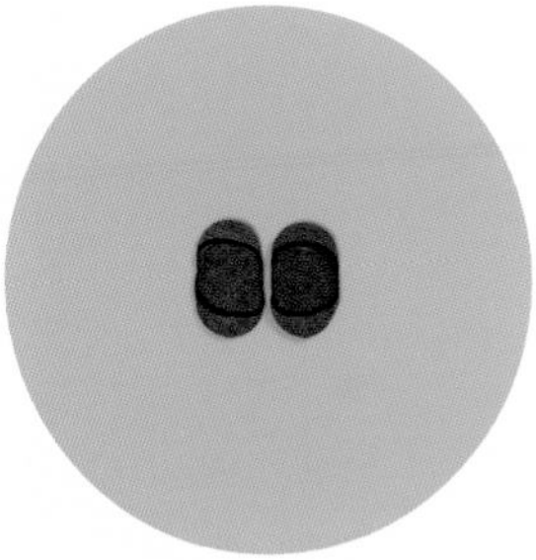

No-Show Socks
44

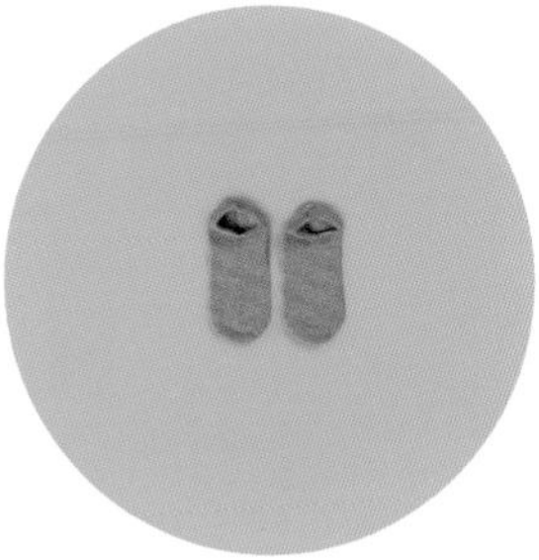

Ankle Socks
45

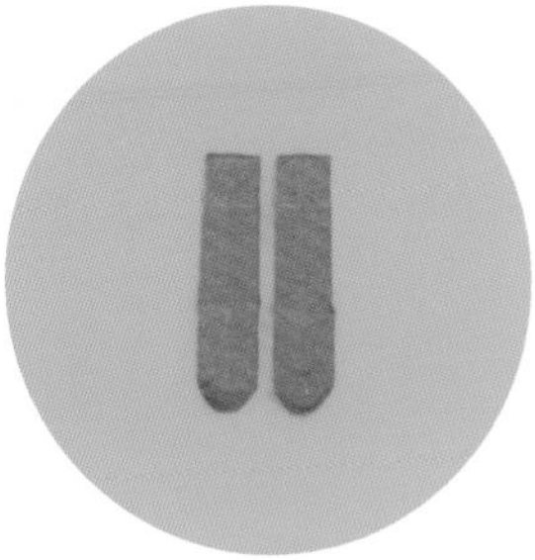

Calf Socks
46

Tank Top

1 Lay the tank top faceup on a flat surface.

2 Fold in the right side to the middle.

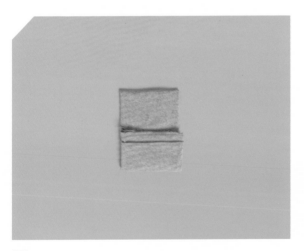

5 Bring up the bottom to the middle.

6 Fold up the bottom again and align with the top.

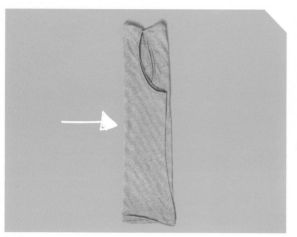

3 Fold in the left side over the right side.

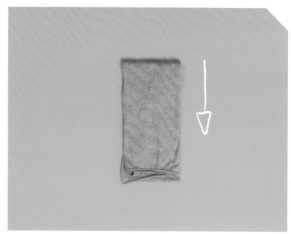

4 Fold in half from top to bottom.

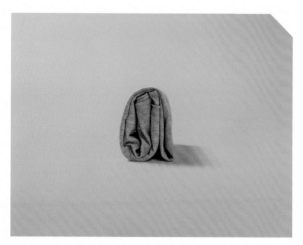

7 Place into a drawer with the rounded edge facing up.

Short-Sleeve T-Shirt

1 Lay the short-sleeve T-shirt facedown on a flat surface.

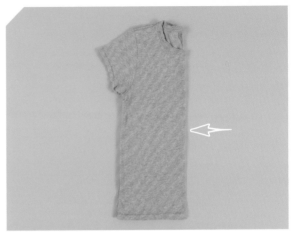

2 Fold in half from right to left.

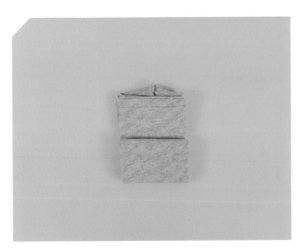

5 Fold up the bottom to the middle.

6 Fold up the bottom a final time and align with the top.

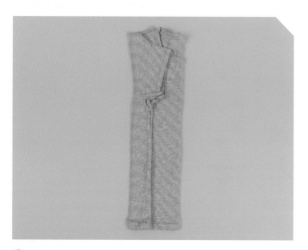

3 Fold the left side inward toward the right side.

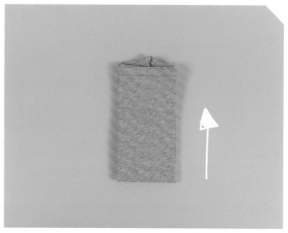

4 Bring up the bottom to right below the neckline.

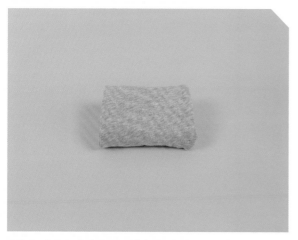

7 Place into a drawer with the rounded edge facing up.

Janelle says . . .

If the shirt has a graphic on it, the graphic side should be facedown in step 1. This way you will see the identifying graphic when it is file-folded in the drawer.

Short-Sleeve T-Shirt (Variation)

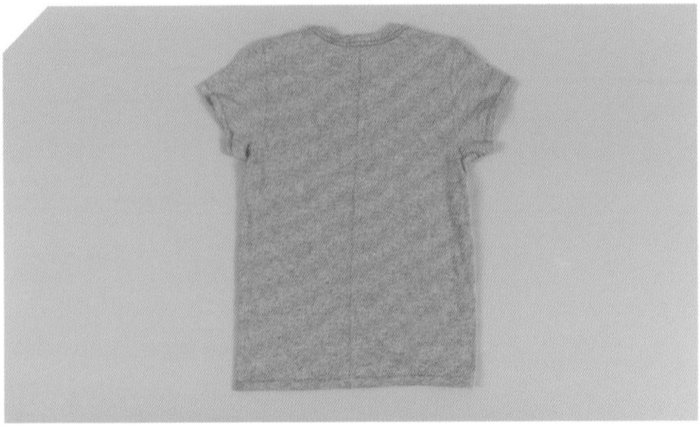

1 Lay the short-sleeve T-shirt facedown on a flat surface.

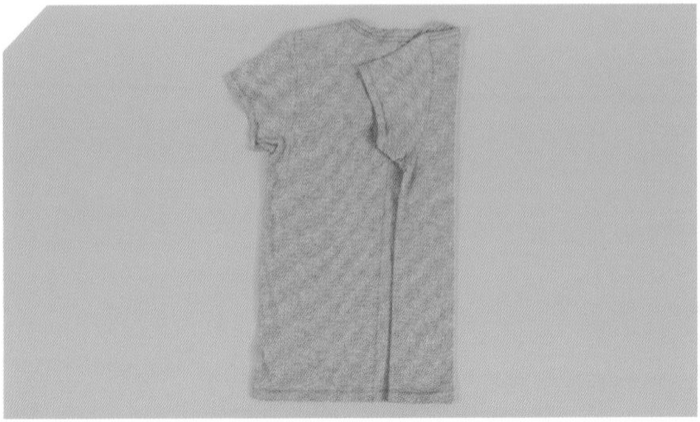

2 Fold in the right side slightly past the right edge of the neckline.

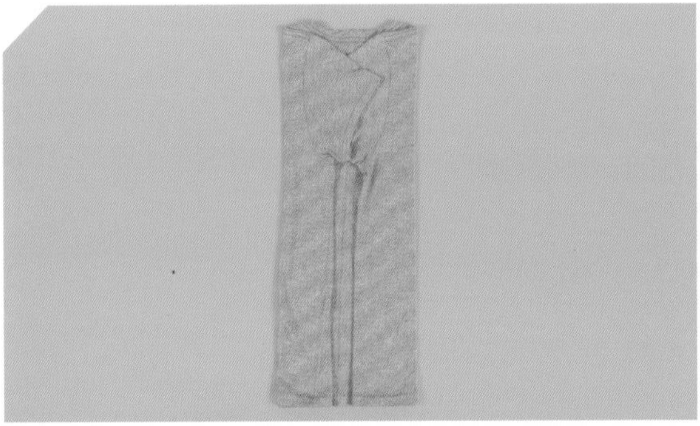

3 Fold in the left side to match the right side. If your shirt is on the wider side, you may need to fold back the sleeves to keep it from becoming too bulky in the middle.

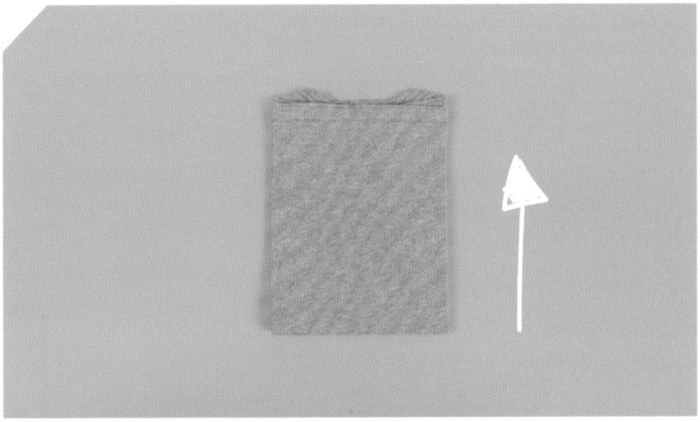

4 Bring up the bottom to right below the neckline.

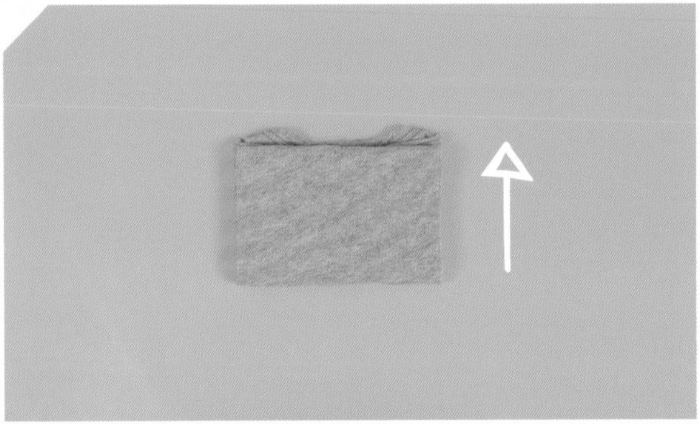

5 Fold in half from bottom to top.

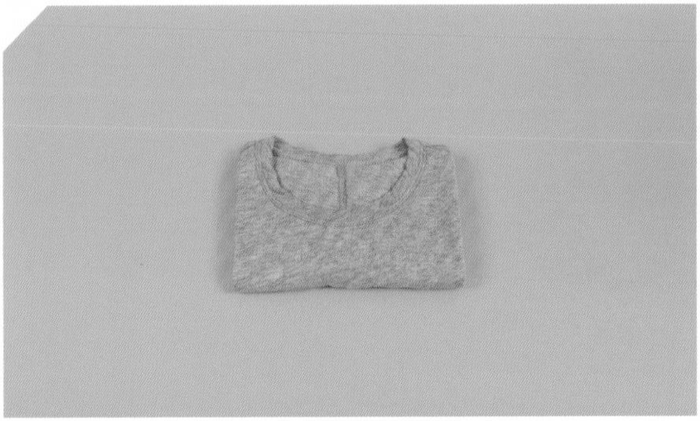

6 Place into a drawer with the rounded edge facing up.

Short-Sleeve Button-Down

1 Lay the short-sleeve button-down facedown on a flat surface.

2 Fold in the right side slightly past the right edge of the collar.

3 Fold in the left side to match the right side.

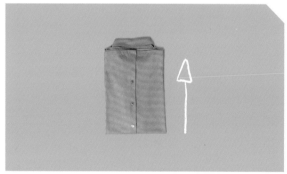

4 Bring up the bottom to right below the collar.

5 To avoid damaging the collar, place on a shelf faceup with the rounded edge facing out.

Janelle says...

The shirt will be easier to fold if it is buttoned. You can button all the buttons, or just the top, middle, and bottom buttons.

Long-Sleeve T-Shirt

1 Lay the long-sleeve T-shirt facedown on a flat surface.

2 Fold in half from right to left.

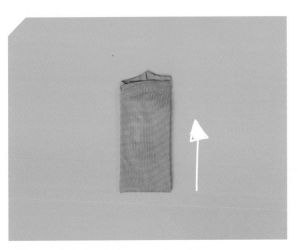

5 Bring up the bottom to right below the neckline.

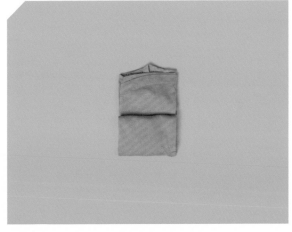

6 Fold up the bottom again to the middle.

Janelle says . . . If your long-sleeve T-shirt has a turtleneck, in step 4, fold down the neck after you fold the sleeves.

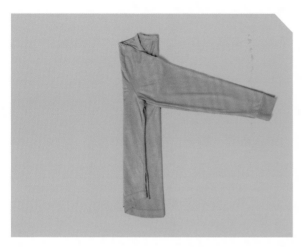

3 Fold the left side back halfway toward the right side.

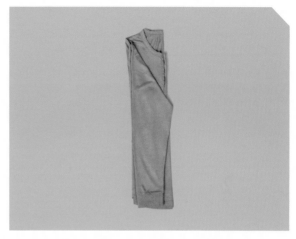

4 Fold the sleeves back and bend them down at the elbows so that they lie flat on the middle of the shirt.

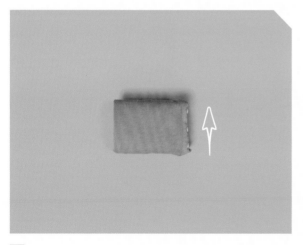

7 Fold up the bottom a final time and align with the top.

8 Place into a drawer with the rounded edge facing up.

Long-Sleeve Button-Down

1 Lay the long-sleeve button-down facedown on a flat surface.

2 Fold in the right side slightly past the right edge of the collar.

5 Fold the left sleeve back, bend it down at the elbow, and lay it on top of the right sleeve.

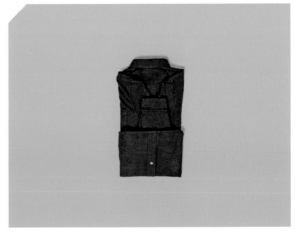

6 Bring up the bottom to the middle.

Janelle says . . . The shirt will be easier to fold if it is buttoned. You can button all the buttons, or just the top, middle, and bottom buttons.

3 Fold the right sleeve back and bend it down at the elbow so that it lies flat on the middle of the shirt.

4 Fold in the left side to match the right side.

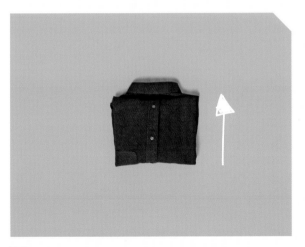

7 Fold up the bottom again to right below the collar.

8 To avoid damaging the collar, place on a shelf faceup with the rounded edge facing out.

Sweater

1 Lay the sweater facedown on a flat surface.

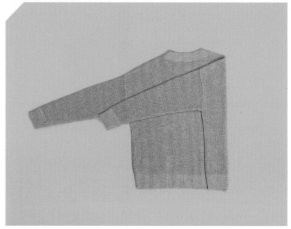

2 Fold in the right side slightly past the right edge of the neckline.

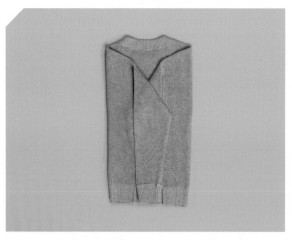

5 Fold the left sleeve back, bend it down at the elbow, and lay it on top of the right sleeve.

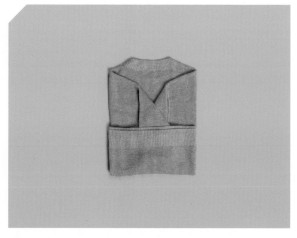

6 Bring up the bottom to the middle.

Janelle says . . . If storing on a shelf, in step 6, fold up the bottom to right below the neckline and place faceup on the shelf with the rounded edge facing out.

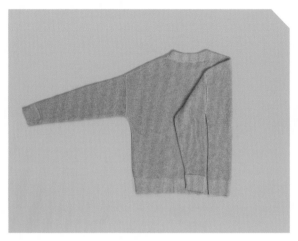

3 Fold the right sleeve back and bend it down at the elbow so that it lies flat on the middle of the sweater.

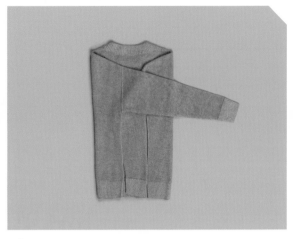

4 Fold in the left side to match the right side.

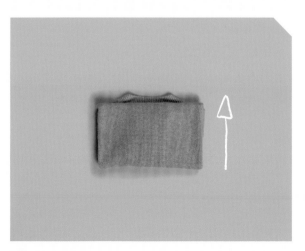

7 Fold up the bottom again to right below the neckline.

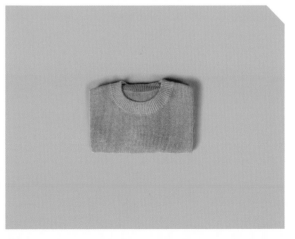

8 Place into a drawer with the rounded edge facing up. If storing on a shelf, see the tip at the top of the page.

Cardigan

1 Lay the cardigan facedown on a flat surface with all the buttons buttoned.

2 Fold in the right side slightly past the right edge of the neckline.

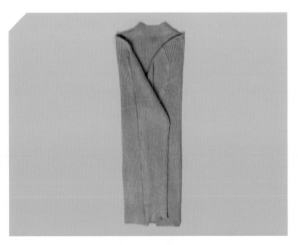

5 Fold the left sleeve back, bend it down at the elbow, and lay it on top of the right sleeve.

6 Bring up the bottom to the middle.

Janelle says . . . If storing on a shelf, in step 6, fold up the bottom to right below the neckline and place faceup on the shelf with the rounded edge facing out.

3 Fold the right sleeve back and bend it down at the elbow so that it lies flat on the middle of the cardigan.

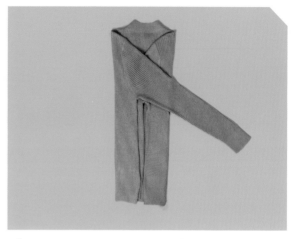

4 Fold in the left side to match the right side.

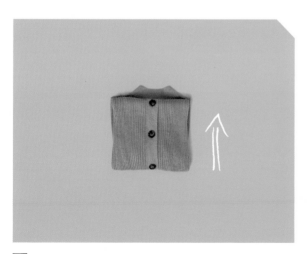

7 Fold up the bottom again to right below the neckline.

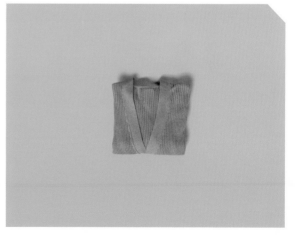

8 Place into a drawer with the rounded edge facing up. If storing on a shelf, see the tip at the top of the page.

Sweatshirt

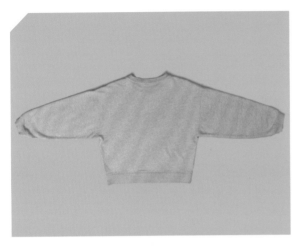

1 Lay the sweatshirt facedown on a flat surface.

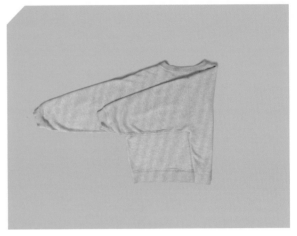

2 Fold in the right side slightly past the right edge of the neckline.

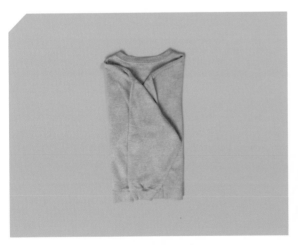

5 Fold the left sleeve back, bend it down at the elbow, and lay it on top of the right sleeve.

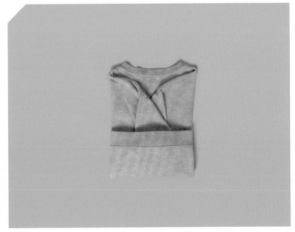

6 Bring up the bottom to the middle.

If storing on a shelf, in step 6, fold up the bottom
to right below the neckline and place faceup on
the shelf with the rounded edge facing out.

Janelle says...

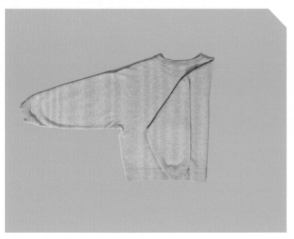

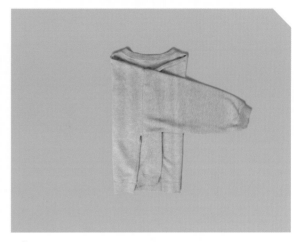

3 Fold the right sleeve back and bend it down at the elbow so that is lies flat on the middle of the sweatshirt.

4 Fold in the left side to match the right side.

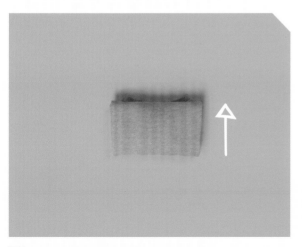

7 Fold up the bottom again and align with the top.

8 Place into a drawer with the rounded edge facing up. If storing on a shelf, see the tip at the top of the page.

Hoodie

1 Lay the hoodie facedown on a flat surface. Make sure the hood is flat. If the hoodie has a zipper, zip it up to make folding easier.

2 Fold in the right side the width of the shoulder.

5 Fold the left sleeve back, bend it down at the elbow, and lay it on top of the right sleeve.

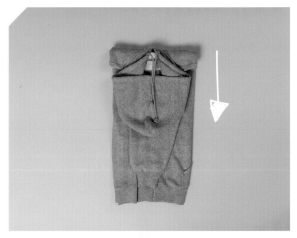

6 Fold down the hood and lay any strings on the hood.

Janelle says... If storing on a shelf, in step 7, fold in half from bottom to top and place faceup on the shelf with the rounded edge facing out.

3 Fold the right sleeve back and bend it down at the elbow so that it lies flat on the middle of the hoodie.

4 Fold in the left side to match the right side.

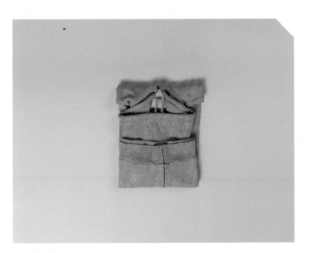

7 Bring up the bottom to the middle.

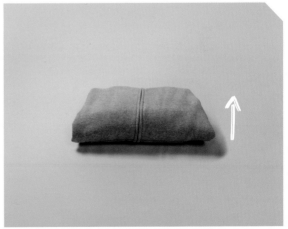

8 Fold up the bottom again and align with the top. Place into a drawer with the rounded edge facing up. If storing on a shelf, see the tip at the top of the page.

Casual Pants/Denim

1 Lay the casual pants faceup on a flat surface.

2 Fold in half from right to left. Notice the little triangle at the booty part of the pants? That's what I call the "booty triangle." Fold it over to create a clean, straight line.

3 Fold up the legs to right below the waistline.

4 Bring up the bottom of the pants to the middle.

5 Fold up the bottom again and align with the top. Place into a drawer with the rounded edge facing up. If storing on a shelf, see the tip at the right.

Janelle says . . .

If storing on a shelf, in step 4, fold in half from bottom to top and place on the shelf with the rounded edge facing out.

Dress Pants (Hanger)

1 Lay the dress pants faceup on a flat surface.

Janelle says...

When storing dress pants on a hanger, make sure the bottoms of the pants are even with the waistband. This will keep the pants balanced on the hanger and help them hang level. Also, when hanging pants in the closet, place the backside toward the wall.

2 Place your thumb and index finger on the two belt loops on either side of the button. Pinch the belt loops together to bring some of the fabric inward.

3 Pinch the fabric at the middle back of the pants, then lift the pants off of the surface. When you do this, your pants should be folded in half vertically.

4 Slide the pants over a hanger, aligning the bottoms of the legs with the waistband.

39

Dress Pants (Shelf)

1 Lay the dress pants faceup on a flat surface.

2 Place your thumb and index finger on the two belt loops on either side of the button. Pinch the belt loops together to bring some of the fabric inward.

3 Pinch the fabric at the middle back of your pants, then lift the pants off of the surface. When you do this, the pants should be folded in half vertically.

> **Janelle says . . .** Notice those creases on the fronts of the pant legs? This folding method will naturally fold the pants at those creases to avoid extra wrinkles.

4 Lay the pants back on the flat surface. Bring up the legs to right below the waistline.

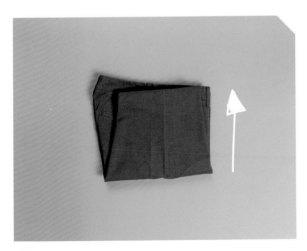

5 Fold in half from bottom to top.

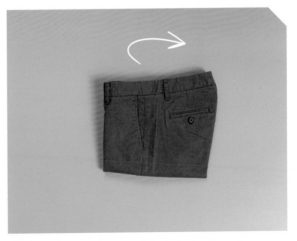

6 Flip the pants over so that the pockets are visible and place on a shelf with the rounded edge facing out.

Sweatpants

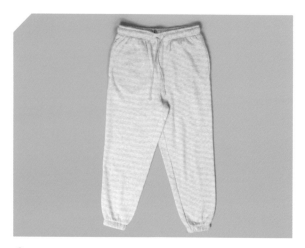

1 Lay the sweatpants faceup on a flat surface.

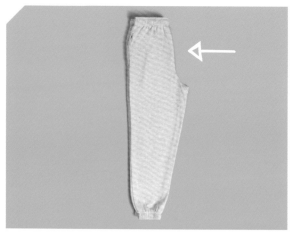

2 Fold in half from right to left.

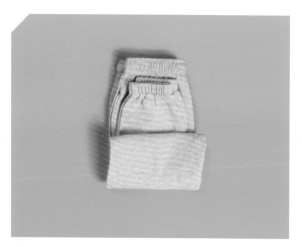

5 Bring up the bottom of the pants to the middle.

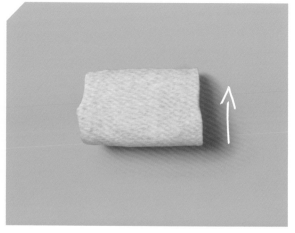

6 Fold up the bottom again and align with the top.

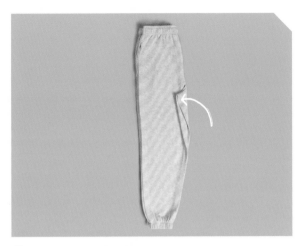

3 Notice the little triangle at the booty part of the sweatpants? That's what I call the "booty triangle." Fold it over to create a clean, straight line.

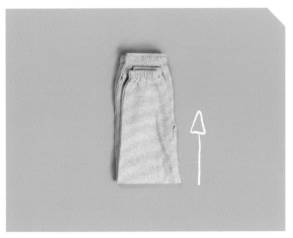

4 Fold up the legs to right below the waistline.

7 Place into a drawer with the rounded edge facing up. If storing on a shelf, see the tip at the right.

Janelle says . . .

If storing on a shelf, in step 5, fold in half from bottom to top and place on the shelf with the rounded edge facing out.

No-Show Socks

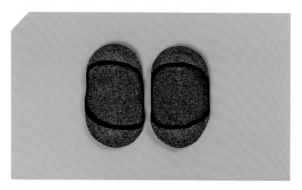

1 Lay the no-show socks on a flat surface with the tops of the socks facing up.

2 Place one sock on top of the other with the top sock halfway down the bottom sock.

3 Fold up the top sock until it aligns with the toe of the bottom sock.

4 Fold up the bottom sock over the top sock.

5 Turn down the opening of the bottom sock and wrap it around the folded parts to create a bundle.

Ankle Socks

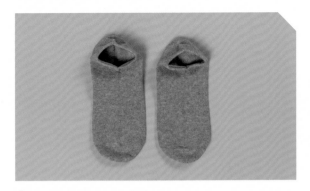

1 Lay the ankle socks on a flat surface with the tops of the socks facing up.

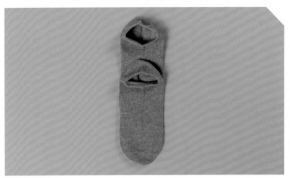

2 Place one sock on top of the other with the top sock below the ankle of the bottom sock.

3 Fold up the top sock until it aligns with the toe of the bottom sock.

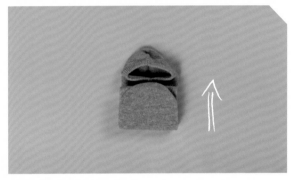

4 Fold up the bottom sock over the top sock.

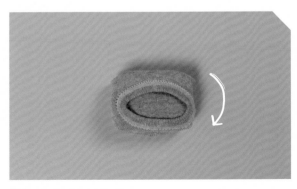

5 Turn down the opening of the bottom sock and wrap it around the folded parts to create a bundle.

45

Calf Socks

1 Lay the calf socks on a flat surface with the tops of the socks facing up.

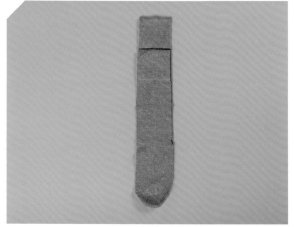

2 Place one sock on top of the other with the top sock one-third of the way down the bottom sock.

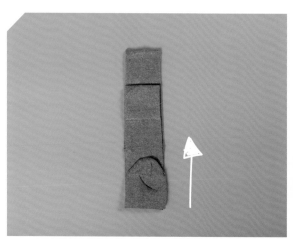

3 Fold up the top sock one-third the length of the sock.

Janelle says . . . You may have been taught to bundle your socks together a different way, but this method really flattens them, doesn't wear out the elastic, and makes a cute little package.

4 Fold up the top sock another third.

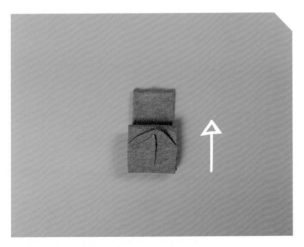

5 Fold up the bottom sock over the top sock.

6 Turn down the opening of the bottom sock and wrap it around the folded parts to create a bundle.

Feminine

Cropped Tank Top
50

Flowy Tank Top
52

Workout Tank Top
54

Tube Top
56

Short-Sleeve Crop Top
57

Cropped Sweatshirt
58

Shorts
60

Bike Shorts
62

Leggings
64

Skirt
66

Skirt (Variation)
68

Pajama Set
69

Nightgown
72

Bodysuit
74

One-Piece Swimsuit
76

Bikini
78

Bralette
80

Padded Bra
81

Sports Bra (Thick Straps)
82

Sports Bra (Thin Adjustable Straps)
83

Bikini Underwear
84

Thong
86

Cropped Tank Top

1 Lay the cropped tank top faceup on a flat surface.

2 Fold in the right side to the middle.

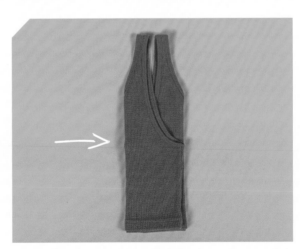

3 Fold in the left side over the right side.

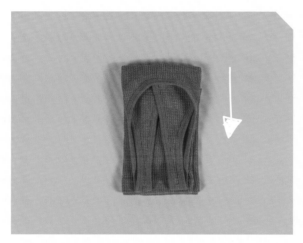

4 Fold in half from top to bottom.

5 Fold in half again, from bottom to top.

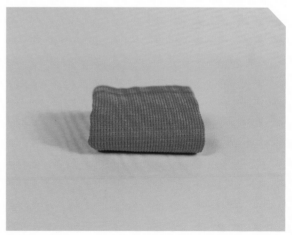

6 Place into a drawer with the rounded edge facing up.

Flowy Tank Top

1 Lay the flowy tank top facedown on a flat surface.

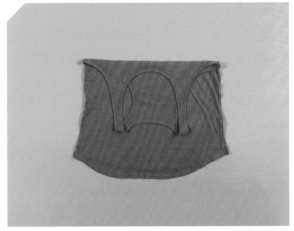

2 Fold down the straps at the base of the armpits to create a straight line across the top.

5 Bring up the bottom to the middle.

6 Fold up the bottom again and align with the top.

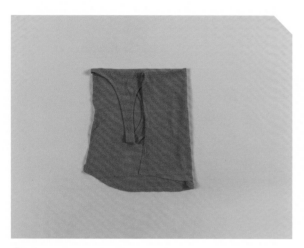

3 Fold in the right side to the middle.

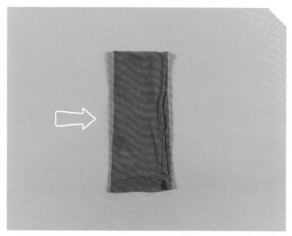

4 Fold in the left side over the right side.

7 Place into a drawer with the rounded edge facing up.

Workout Tank Top

1 Lay the workout tank top facedown on a flat surface.

2 Fold down the straps at the base of the armpits to create a straight line across the top.

5 Bring up the bottom to the middle.

6 Fold up the bottom again and align with the top.

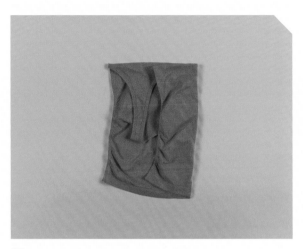

3 Fold in the right side to the middle.

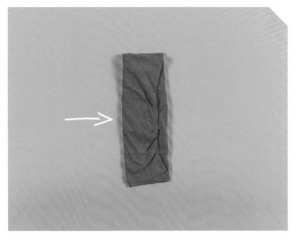

4 Fold in the left side over the right side.

7 Place into a drawer with the rounded edge facing up.

Tube Top

1 Lay the tube top faceup on a flat surface.

2 Fold in the right side to the middle.

3 Fold in the left side over the right side.

4 Fold in half from bottom to top.

5 Place into a drawer with the rounded edge facing up.

Short-Sleeve Crop Top

1 Lay the short-sleeve crop top facedown on a flat surface.

2 Fold in the right side slightly past the right edge of the neckline.

3 Fold in the left side to match the right side.

4 Fold in half from bottom to top.

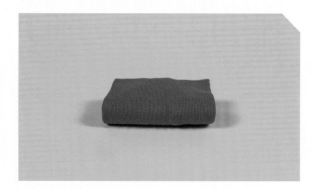

5 Place into a drawer with the rounded edge facing up.

Cropped Sweatshirt

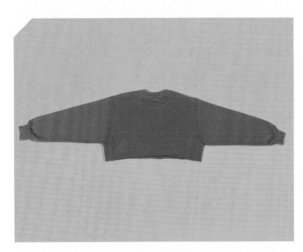

1 Lay the cropped sweatshirt facedown on a flat surface.

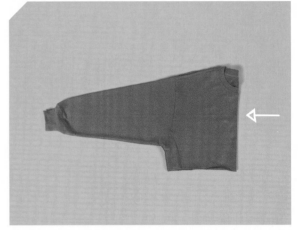

2 Fold in half from right to left, making sure the sleeves are neatly aligned.

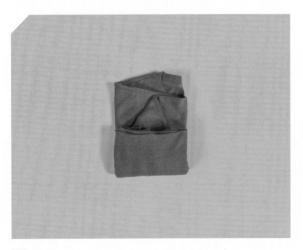

5 Bring up the bottom to the middle.

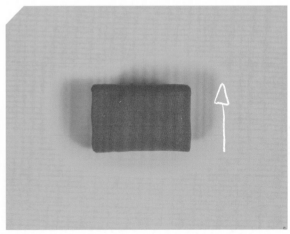

6 Fold up the bottom again and align with the top.

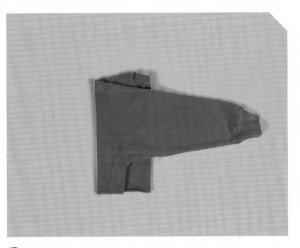

3 Fold the left side back halfway toward the right side.

4 Fold the sleeves back and bend them down at the elbows so that they lie flat on the middle of the sweatshirt.

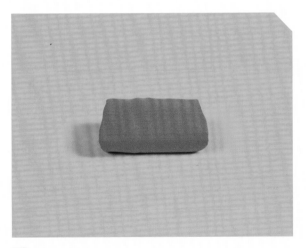

7 Place into a drawer with the rounded edge facing up.

Janelle says . . .

If the sweatshirt has a hood, in step 2, after folding the sweatshirt and hood in half, fold the hood down and lay any strings on top.

Shorts

1 Lay the shorts faceup on a flat surface.

2 Fold in half from right to left.

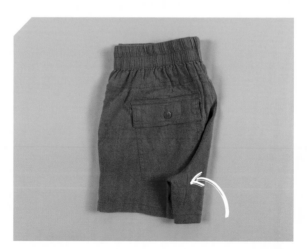

3 Notice the little triangle at the booty part of the shorts? I call that the "booty triangle." Fold it over to create a clean, straight line.

Janelle says... If storing on a shelf, in step 4, fold up the bottom to right below the top of the waistline and place on the shelf with the rounded edge facing out.

4 Bring up the bottom to the middle.

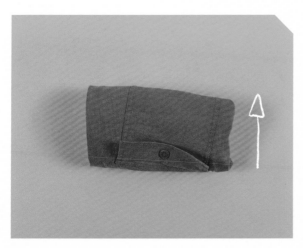

5 Fold up the bottom again and align with the top.

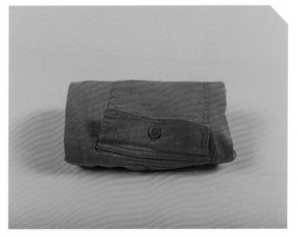

6 Place into a drawer with the rounded edge facing up. If storing on a shelf, see the tip at the top of the page.

Bike Shorts

1 Lay the bike shorts faceup on a flat surface.

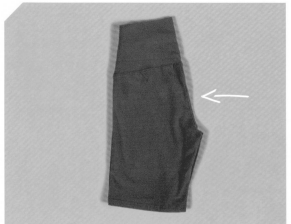

2 Fold in half from right to left.

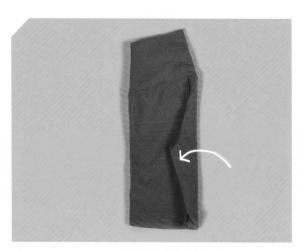

3 Notice the little triangle at the booty part of the shorts? I call that the "booty triangle." Fold it over to create a clean, straight line.

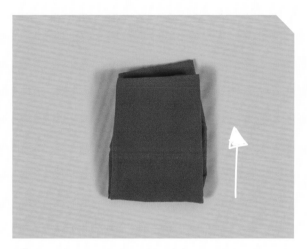

4 Fold up the bottom to right below the top of the waistline.

5 Fold in half from bottom to top.

6 Place into a drawer with the rounded edge facing up.

Leggings

1 Lay the leggings faceup on a flat surface.

2 Fold in half from right to left.

5 Bring up the bottom of the leggings to the middle.

6 Fold up the bottom again and align with the top.

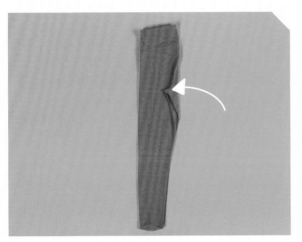

3 Notice the little triangle at the booty part of the leggings? I call that the "booty triangle." Fold it over to create a clean, straight line.

4 Fold up the bottoms to right below the top of the waistline.

7 Place into a drawer with the rounded edge facing up.

Skirt

1 Lay the skirt faceup on a flat surface.

2 Fold in right side to the middle.

5 You have now created a pocket at the waistband.

6 Tuck the bottom of the skirt inside the pocket.

3 Fold in the left side over the right side.

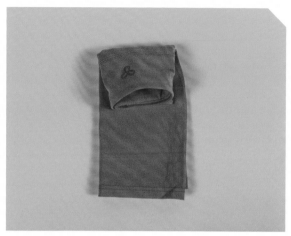

4 Fold down the waistband.

7 Place into a drawer with the pocket opening facing down.

Janelle says...

If a skirt's fabric wrinkles easily, hang the skirt instead of folding it. For a variation on folding a skirt, see page 68.

Skirt (Variation)

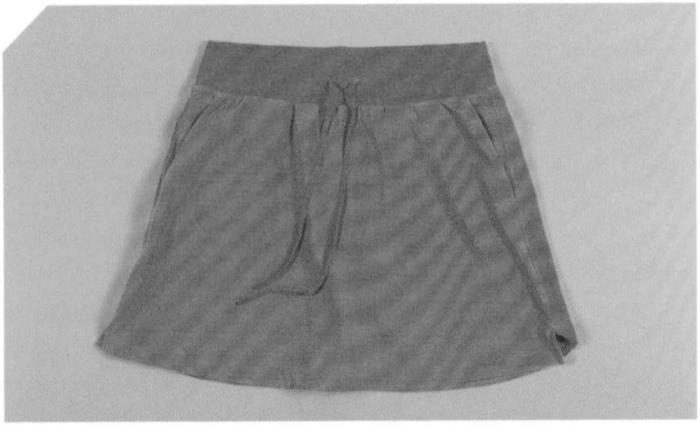

1 Lay the skirt faceup on a flat surface.

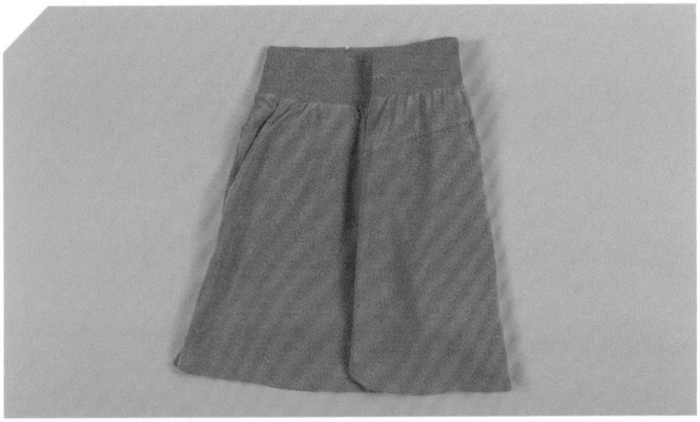

2 Fold in the right side to the middle.

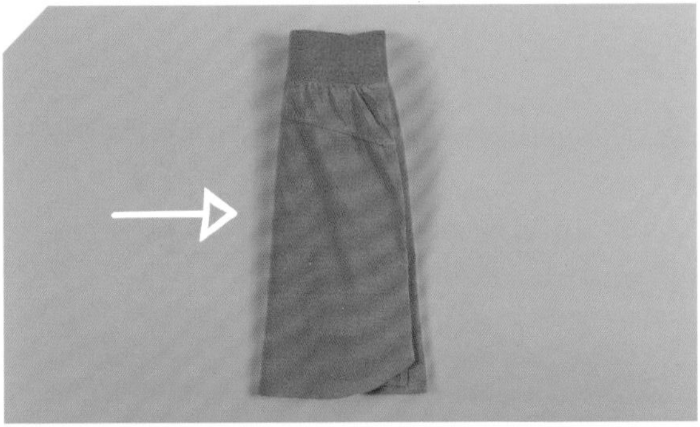

3 Fold in the left side over the right side.

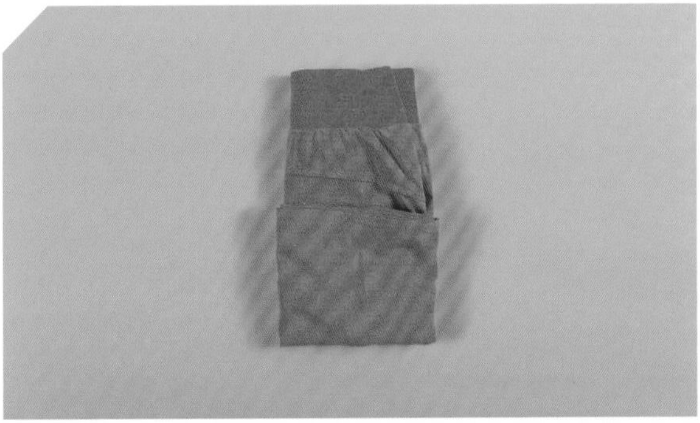

4 Bring up the bottom to the middle.

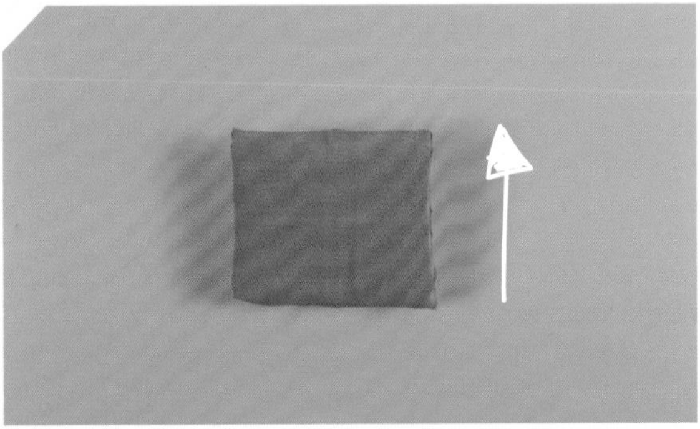

5 Fold up the bottom again and align with the top.

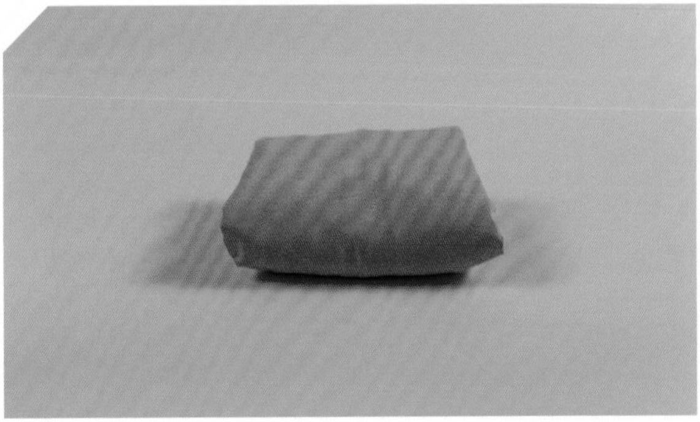

6 Place into a drawer with the rounded edge facing up.

Pajama Set

1 Starting with the pajama shorts, lay them faceup on a flat surface.

2 Fold them in half from right to left.

3 Notice the little triangle at the booty part of the shorts? I call that the "booty triangle." Fold it over to create a clean, straight line.

4 Fold up the bottom to the middle.

5 Bring up the bottom and align with the top. Set aside.

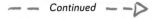

– – Continued – – ▷

69

6 Moving on to the pajama shirt, lay it facedown on the flat surface.

7 Fold in the right side to the middle.

10 Bring up the bottom of the shirt to right below the collar.

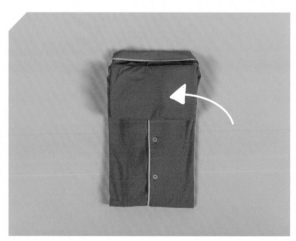

11 Place the folded shorts on the shirt right below the collar.

Janelle says... Pajamas of any sleeve and pant length can be folded together! Just use the folding method in this book for the style of shirt and pants, and then follow steps 10 and 11 to fold them together.

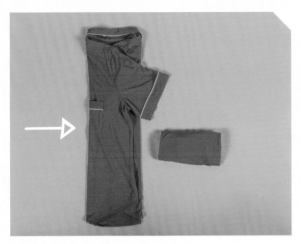

8 Fold in the left side over the right side.

9 Fold back the left sleeve so that it lies flat on the middle of the shirt.

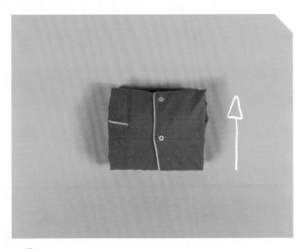

12 Fold in half from bottom to top, with the folded shorts tucked inside.

13 Place into a drawer with the rounded edge facing up.

Nightgown

1 Lay the nightgown facedown on a flat surface.

2 Fold in half from right to left.

5 Bring down the top to the middle.

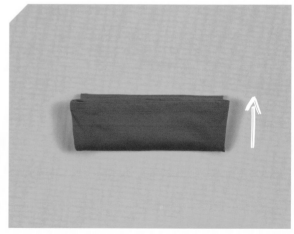

6 Fold the bottom up over the top.

3 Fold down the straps and the top of the nightgown to create a straight line across the top.

4 Fold in half from top to bottom.

7 Fold in half from right to left.

8 Place into a drawer with the rounded edge facing up.

Bodysuit

1 Lay the bodysuit facedown on a flat surface.

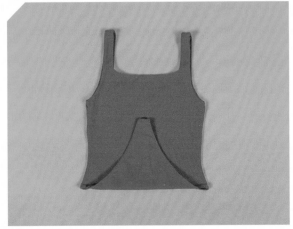

2 Fold up the bottom to create a straight line across the bottom.

5 Fold in the left side over the right side.

6 Fold in half from bottom to top.

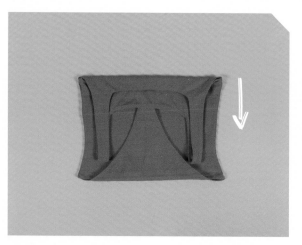

3 Fold down the straps at the base of the armpits to create a straight line across the top.

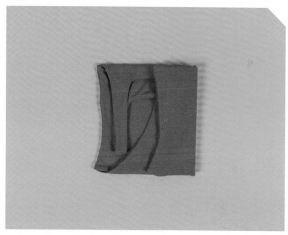

4 Fold in the right side to the middle.

7 Place into a drawer with the rounded edge facing up.

Janelle says...

Adjust this fold as needed depending on the bodysuit's sleeve length. If there are sleeves, in step 1, fold them inward so that they lie flat on the middle of the bodysuit.

One-Piece Swimsuit

1 Lay the one-piece swimsuit facedown on a flat surface.

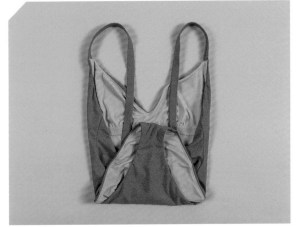

2 Fold up the bottom to create a straight line across the bottom.

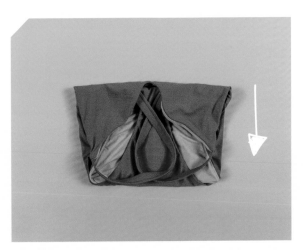

3 Fold down the straps at the base of the armpits to create a straight line across the top.

Janelle says... Adjust this fold as needed, depending on the swimsuit's sleeve length. The goal for any one-piece swimsuit style is to get the shape into a rectangle in step 3 to make it easier to fold.

4 Fold in the right side to the middle.

5 Fold in the left side over the right side.

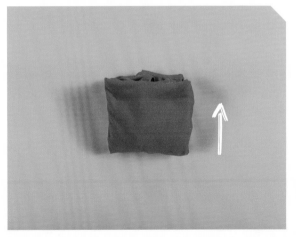

6 Fold in half from bottom to top. Place into a drawer with the rounded edge facing up.

Bikini

1 Starting with the bikini bottom, lay it faceup on a flat surface.

2 Fold in the right side to the middle.

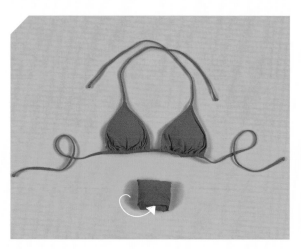

5 You have now created a pocket at the top (see step 4 photo on page 187 for a visual). Tuck the bottom section inside the pocket. Set aside.

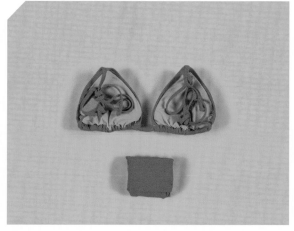

6 Moving to the bikini top, lay it facedown on the flat surface. Tie each strap into a loose knot and tuck them into the cups.

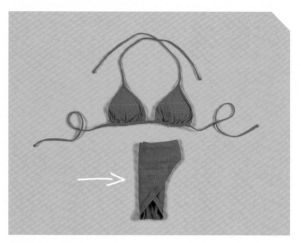

3 Fold the left side over the right side, overcrossing it at the top.

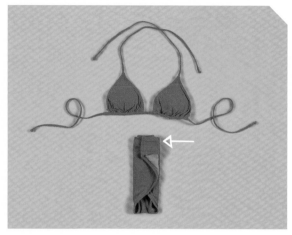

4 Fold back the top left side so that that it aligns with the right edge.

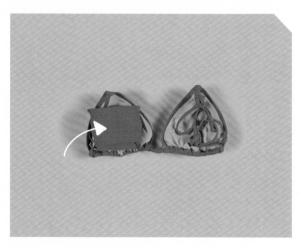

7 Place the folded bikini bottom into the left cup.

8 Fold the right cup over the left cup, creating a bikini sandwich. Place into a drawer with the top of the bikini facing up.

Bralette

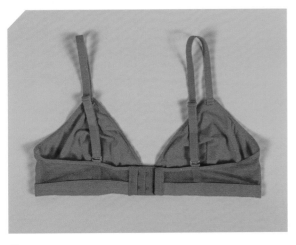

1 Fasten the bralette and lay it facedown on a flat surface.

2 Fold down the straps and tops of the cups to create straight lines across the tops. Tuck the straps into the cups.

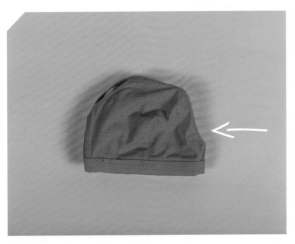

3 Fold over the right cup to cover the left cup.

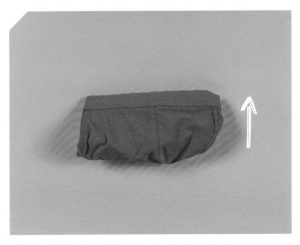

4 Fold in half from bottom to top. Place into a drawer with the rounded edge facing up.

Janelle says... Instead of filing these bras upright in a drawer, you can lay them in a row, slightly overlapping one another so that each bra is visible.

Padded Bra

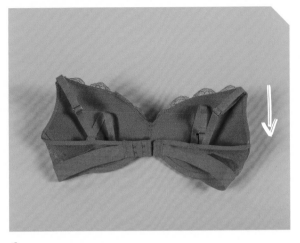

1 Fasten the padded bra and lay it facedown on a flat surface. Tuck the straps into the cups.

2 Fold the right cup over the left cup.

3 Push in the left cup to nest inside the right cup.

4 Place into a drawer with the top of the bra facing up.

Janelle says . . . To preserve your bras as long as possible, instead of folding them, you can lay them flat, one on top of the other, but if you need to save space, the method above is a great solution.

Sports Bra (Thick Straps)

1 Lay the sports bra facedown on a flat surface.

2 Fold in half from top to bottom.

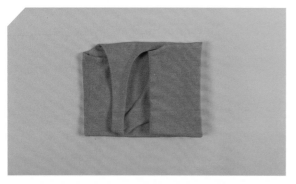

3 Fold in the right side to the middle.

4 Fold in the left side over the right side.

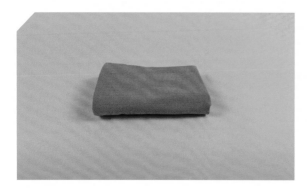

5 Place into a drawer with the rounded edge facing up.

Janelle says...

Instead of filing these bras upright in a drawer, you can lay them in a row, slightly overlapping one another so that each bra is visible.

Sports Bra (Thin Adjustable Straps)

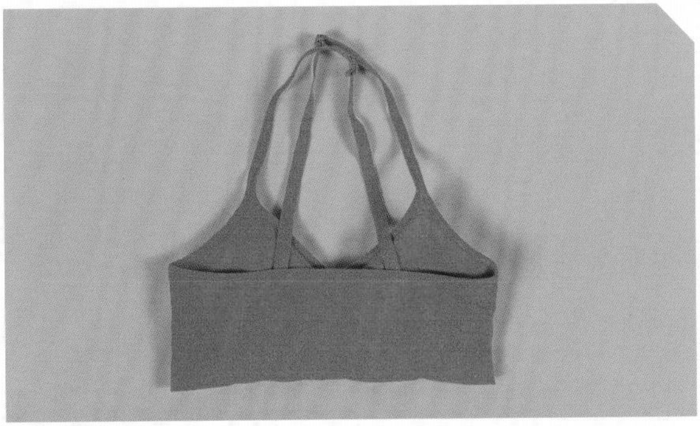

1 Lay the sports bra facedown on a flat surface.

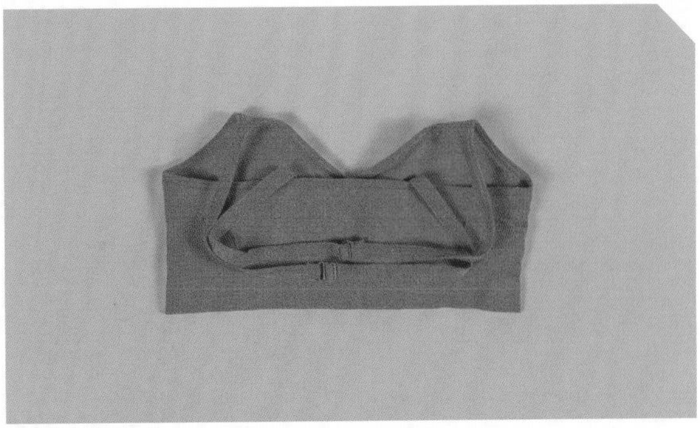

2 Fold down the straps and tops of the cups to create straight lines across the tops.

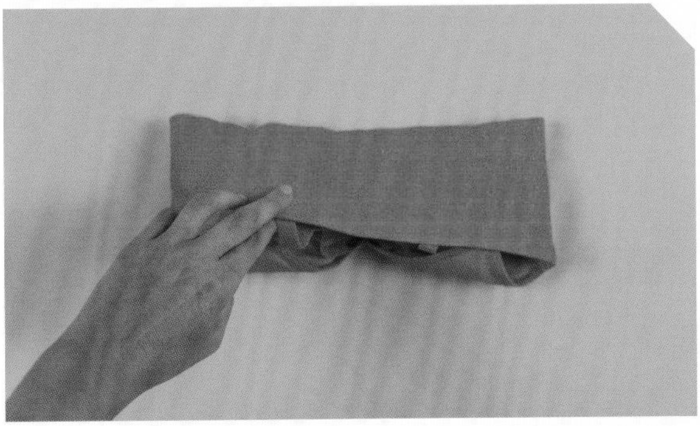

3 Tuck the straps into the cups.

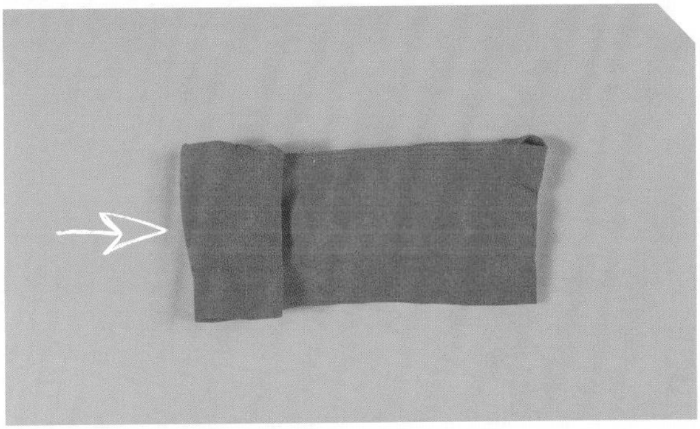

4 Fold in the left side one-third the width of the bra.

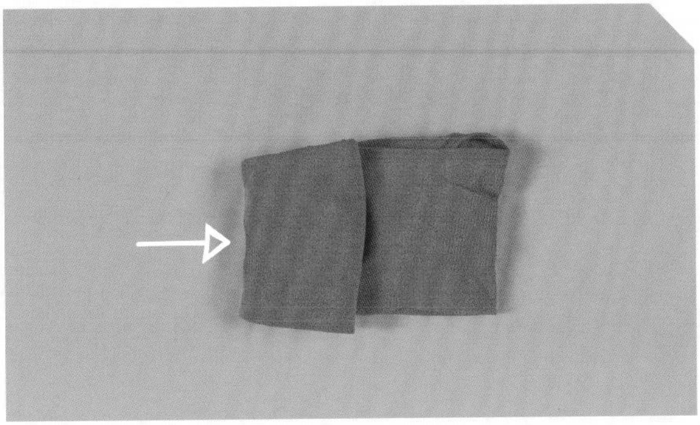

5 Fold in the left side another third.

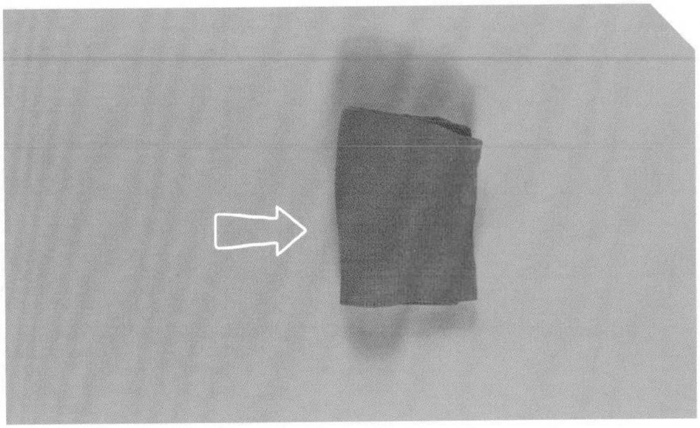

6 Fold in the left side the final third and align with the right side. Place into a drawer with the rounded edge facing up.

Bikini Underwear

1 Lay the bikini underwear faceup on a flat surface.

2 Fold in the right side to the middle.

5 Fold back the top-left side so that that it aligns with the right edge.

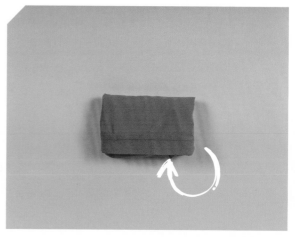

6 You have now created a pocket at the top (see step 4 photo on page 187 for a visual). Tuck the bottom section inside the pocket.

3 Fold back the top-right side halfway.

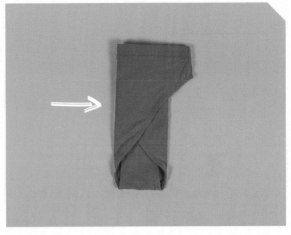

4 Fold the left side over the right side, overcrossing it at the top.

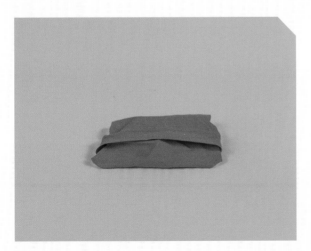

7 Place into a drawer with the pocket opening facing down.

Thong

1 Lay the thong facedown on a flat surface.

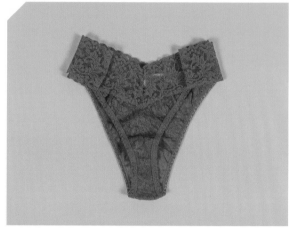

2 Fold in both sides of the waistband so that they align with the edges of the leg openings.

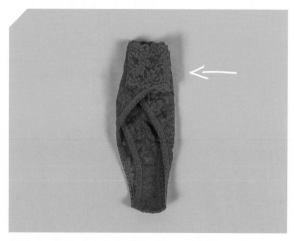

5 Fold back the waistband.

6 You have now created a pocket at the top.

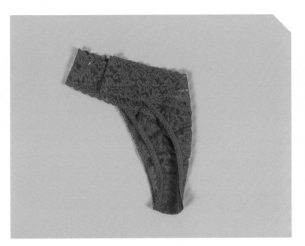

3 Fold in the right side to the middle.

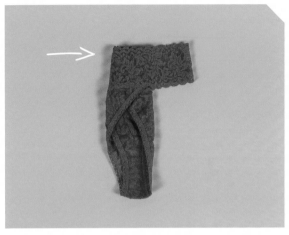

4 Fold in the left side to match the right side, overcrossing the right side at the top.

7 Tuck the bottom section inside the pocket.

8 Place into a drawer with the pocket opening facing down.

Masculine

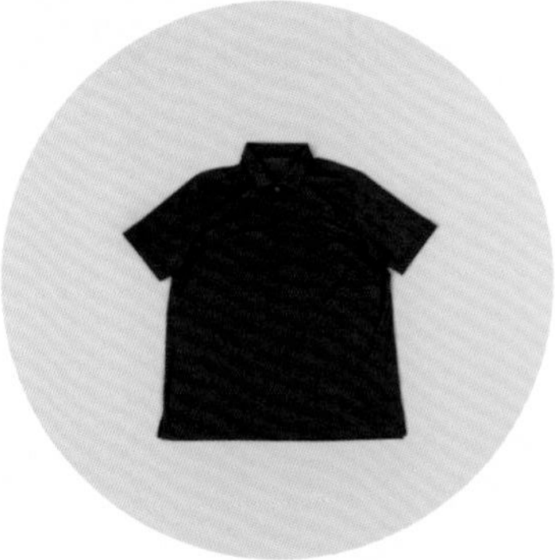

Polo Shirt
90

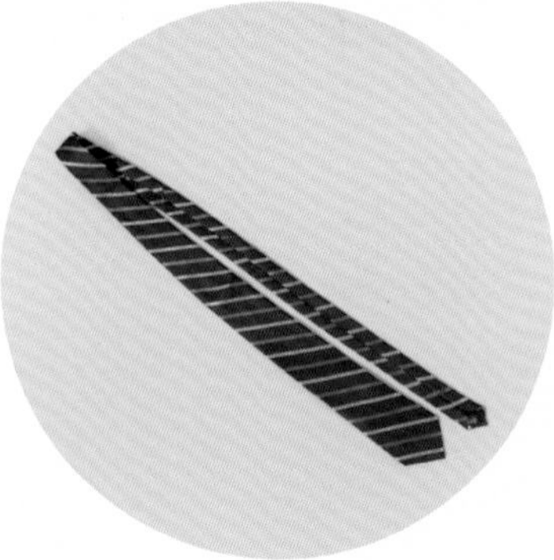

Tie
92

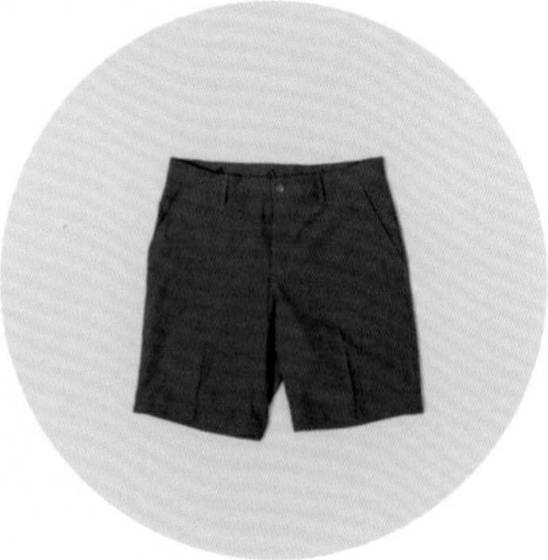

Shorts
93

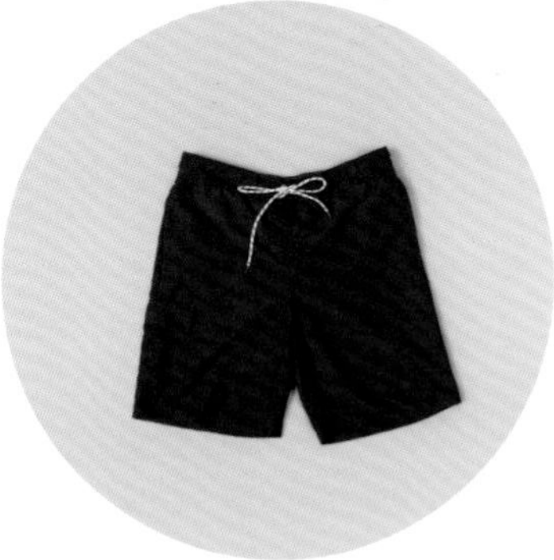

Swim Trunks
94

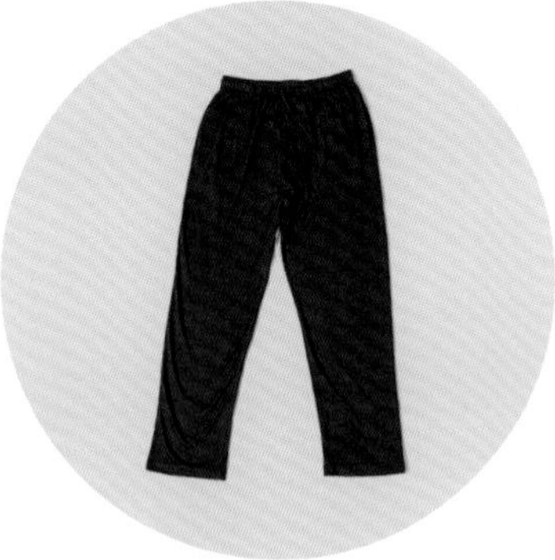

Pajama Bottoms
96

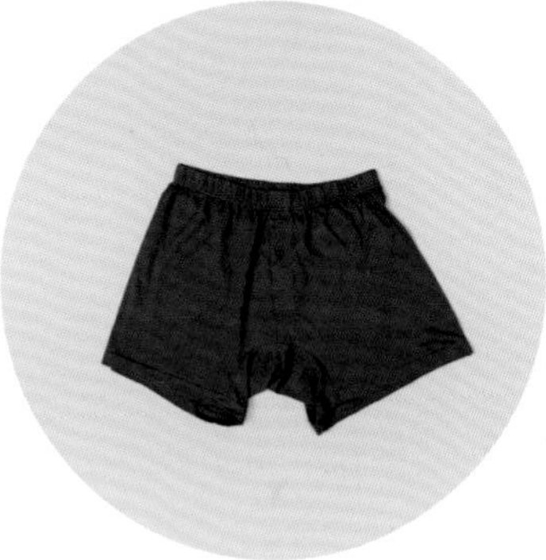

Boxers
98

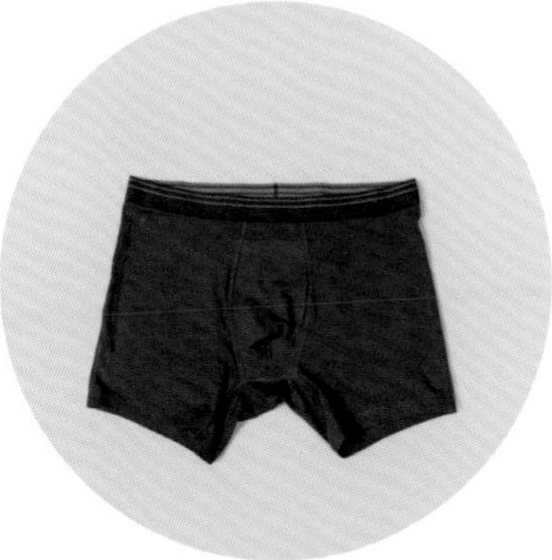

Boxer Briefs
99

Polo Shirt

1 Lay the polo shirt facedown on a flat surface.

2 Fold in the right side slightly past the right edge of the collar.

3 Fold in the left side to match the right side. Fold back the left sleeve if it overcrosses the right side.

Janelle says . . . The shirt will be easier to fold if it is buttoned. You can button all the buttons, or just the top one.

4 Bring up the bottom to the middle.

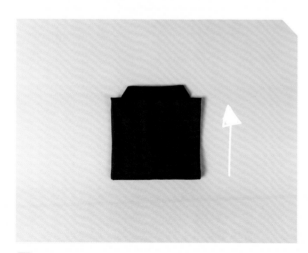

5 Fold up the bottom again to right below the collar.

6 To avoid damaging the collar, place on a shelf faceup with the rounded edge facing out.

Tie

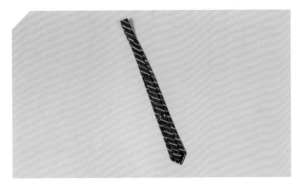

1 Lay the tie facedown on a flat surface. Fold in half from top to bottom, with the back side secured in the loop on the back of the tie.

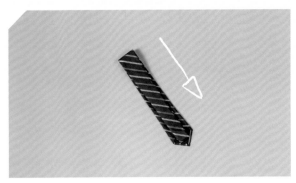

2 Fold in half from top to bottom.

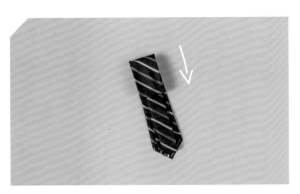

3 Bring down the top to the middle.

4 Fold down the top and align with the bottom.

5 Place into a drawer with the rounded edge (non-pointy side) facing up.

Shorts

1 Lay the shorts faceup on a flat surface.

2 Fold in half from right to left.

3 Notice the little triangle at the booty part of the shorts? That's what I call the "booty triangle." Fold it over to create a clean, straight line.

4 Fold up the bottom to right below the waistline.

5 Place on a shelf with the rounded edge facing out. If storing in a drawer, see the tip at the right.

Janelle says . . .

If storing in a drawer, follow the folding method for Swim Trunks on page 94.

Swim Trunks

1 Lay the swim trunks faceup on a flat surface.

2 Fold in half from right to left.

3 Notice the little triangle at the booty part of the swim trunks? That's what I call the "booty triangle." Fold it over to create a clean, straight line.

4 Bring up the bottom to the middle.

5 Fold up the bottom again and align with the top.

6 Place into a drawer with the rounded edge facing up.

Pajama Bottoms

1 Lay the pajama bottoms faceup on a flat surface.

2 Fold in half from right to left.

5 Bring up the bottom of the pajama bottoms to the middle.

6 Fold up the bottom again to right below the waistline.

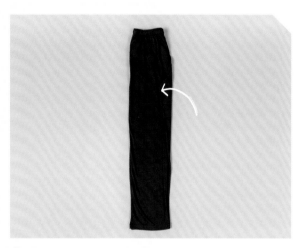

3 Notice the little triangle at the booty part of the bottoms? I call that the "booty triangle." Fold it over to create a clean, straight line.

4 Fold up the legs to right below the waistline.

7 Place into a drawer with the rounded edge facing up.

Janelle says...

This folding method also works for athletic pants.

Boxers

1 Lay the boxers faceup on a flat surface.

2 Fold in the right side to the middle.

3 Fold in the left side over the right side.

4 Flip the boxers over. (Trust me; it helps.) You have now created a pocket at the top.

5 Tuck the legs inside the pocket. Place into a drawer with the pocket opening facing down.

Boxer Briefs

1 Lay the boxer briefs faceup on a flat surface.

2 Fold in the right side to the middle.

3 Fold in the left side over the right side.

4 Flip the boxers over. (Trust me; it helps.) You have now created a pocket at the top.

5 Tuck the legs inside the pocket. Place into a drawer with the pocket opening facing down.

Baby

Sleeveless Onesie
102

Short-Sleeve Onesie
104

Sleeveless Romper
106

Short-Sleeve Romper
108

Pajamas
110

Short-Sleeve T-Shirt
112

Sweatshirt
114

Bloomers
116

Shorts
117

Pants
118

Leggings
120

Sweatpants
122

Overalls
123

Dress
124

Sweat Suit
126

Two-Piece Swimsuit
129

One-Piece Swimsuit
132

Swim Trunks
134

Socks
135

Beanie
136

Bib
137

Bandana Bib
138

Hooded Towel
140

Burp Cloth
142

Muslin Blanket
144

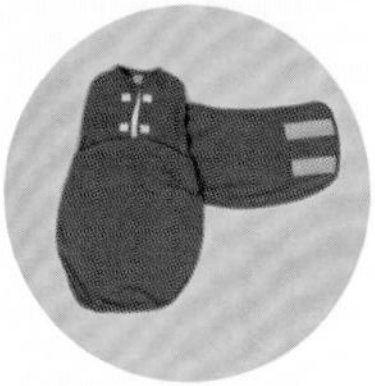

Sleep Sack
146

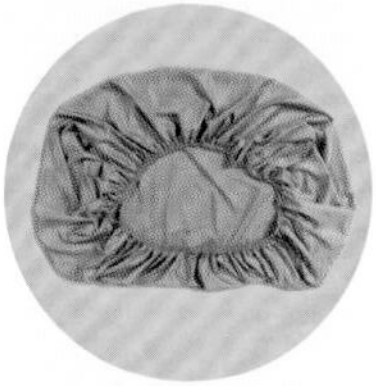

Crib Sheet
148

Sleeveless Onesie

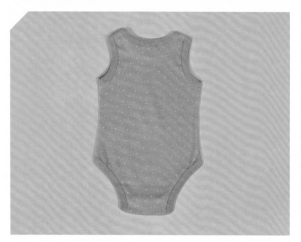

1 Lay the sleeveless onesie facedown on a flat surface.

2 Fold in the right side to the middle.

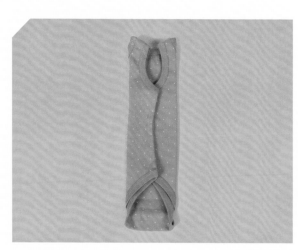

3 Fold in the left side, slightly overlapping the right side.

Janelle says... Always snap or fasten buttons and zip zippers to make folding baby clothes easier.

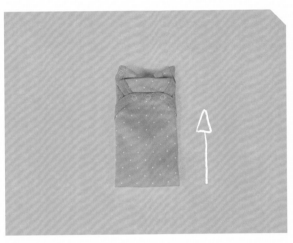

4 Bring up the bottom and align with the top of the neckline.

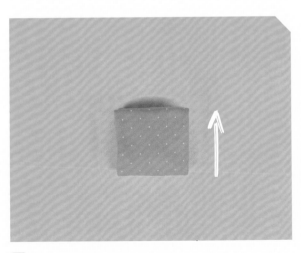

5 Fold in half from bottom to top.

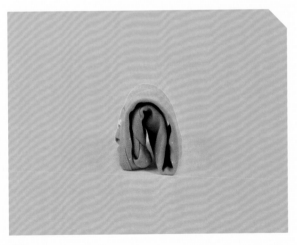

6 Place into a drawer with the rounded edge facing up.

Short-Sleeve Onesie

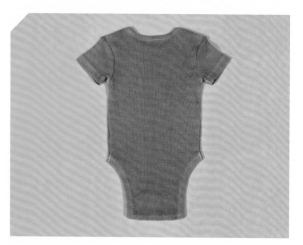

1 Lay the short-sleeve onesie facedown on a flat surface. Start with the onesie snapped closed for easier folding.

2 Fold in the right side toward the middle.

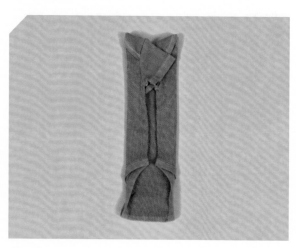

3 Fold in the left side to match the right side.

Janelle says . . . To fold a long-sleeve onesie, follow steps 2 to 5 for Sweatshirt on page 114 for folding the sleeves.

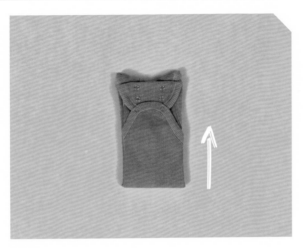

4 Bring up the bottom and align with the top of the neckline.

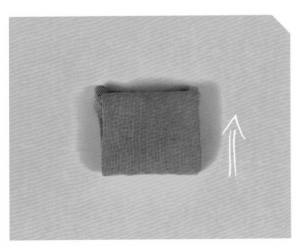

5 Fold in half from bottom to top.

6 Place into a drawer with the rounded edge facing up.

Sleeveless Romper

1 Lay the sleeveless romper facedown on a flat surface. Start with the romper snapped closed for easier folding.

2 Fold in half from right to left.

3 Fold up the legs to the base of the armpit.

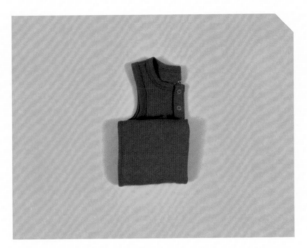

4 Bring up the bottom to the middle.

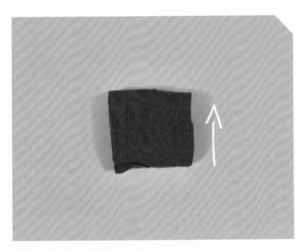

5 Fold up the bottom again and align with the top.

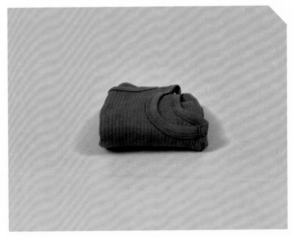

6 Place into a drawer with the rounded edge facing up.

Short-Sleeve Romper

1 Lay the short-sleeve romper facedown on a flat surface. Start with the romper zipped (or snapped) closed for easier folding.

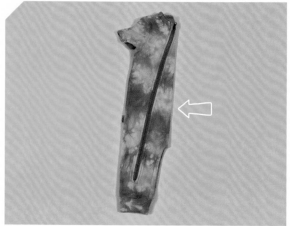

2 Fold in half from right to left.

5 Bring up the bottom to the middle.

6 Fold up the bottom again and align with the top.

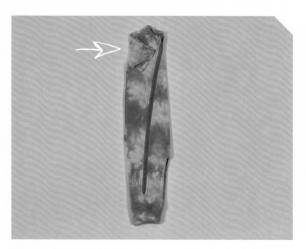

3 Fold back the sleeves over the romper body.

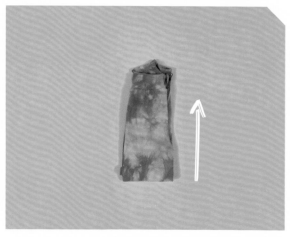

4 Fold up the legs to right below the neckline.

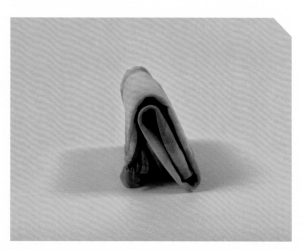

7 Place into a drawer with the rounded edge facing up.

Janelle says . . .

For a long-sleeve romper,
see the folding method for
Pajamas on page 110.

Pajamas

1 Lay the pajamas facedown on a flat surface. Start with the pajamas snapped closed for easier folding.

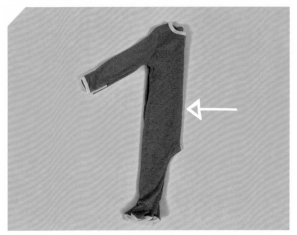

2 Fold in half from right to left, making sure the sleeves are neatly aligned.

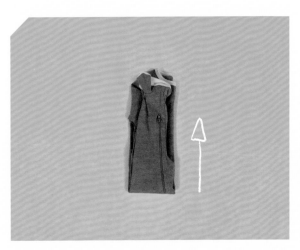

5 Fold up the feet to right below the neckline.

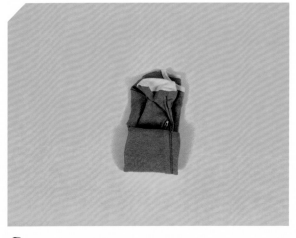

6 Bring up the bottom to the middle.

Janelle says... You can also use this folding method for long-sleeve rompers.

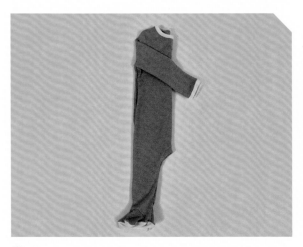

3 Fold the sleeves back across the right side.

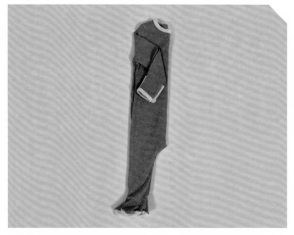

4 Bend the sleeves down at the elbows so that they lie flat on the middle of the romper.

7 Fold up the bottom again and align with the top.

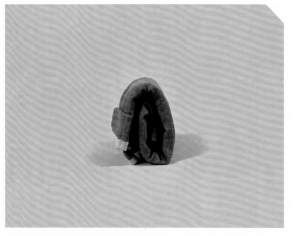

8 Place into a drawer with the rounded edge facing up.

Short-Sleeve T-Shirt

1 Lay the short-sleeve T-shirt facedown on a flat surface.

2 Fold in the right side toward the middle.

3 Fold in the left side to match the right side.

Janelle says... If the shirt has a graphic on it, the graphic side should be facedown in step 1. This way you will see the identifying graphic when it is file-folded in the drawer.

4 Bring up the bottom to the middle.

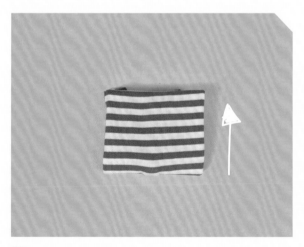

5 Fold up the bottom again and align with the top.

6 Place into a drawer with the rounded edge facing up.

Sweatshirt

1 Lay the sweatshirt facedown on a flat surface.

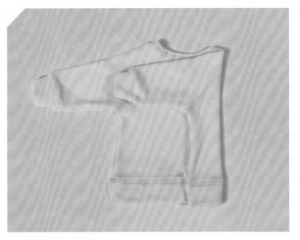

2 Fold in the right side slightly past the right edge of the neckline.

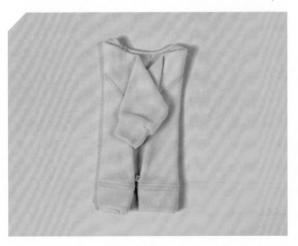

5 Fold the left sleeve back, bend it down at the elbow, and lay it on top of the right sleeve.

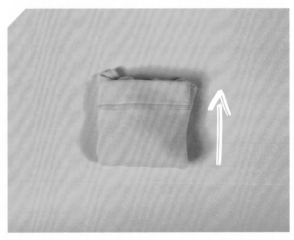

6 Fold in half from bottom to top.

3 Fold the right sleeve back and bend it down at the elbow so that it lies flat on the middle of the sweatshirt.

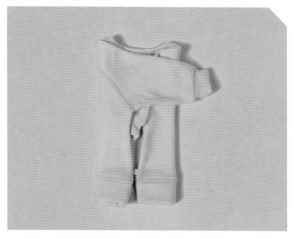

4 Fold in the left side to match the right side.

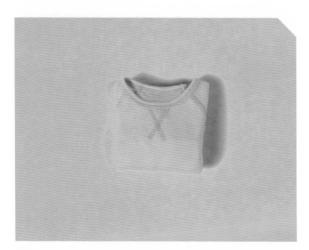

7 Place into a drawer with the rounded edge facing up.

Janelle says . . .

See page 126 to learn how to fold a sweat suit into a set.

Bloomers

1 Lay the bloomers faceup on a flat surface.

2 Fold in the right side to the middle.

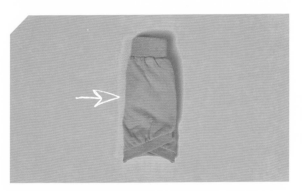

3 Fold the left side over the right side.

4 Fold in half from bottom to top.

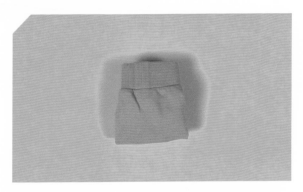

5 Place into a drawer with the rounded edge facing up.

Shorts

1 Lay the shorts faceup on a flat surface.

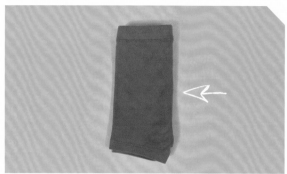

2 Fold in half from right to left.

3 Notice the little triangle at the booty part of the shorts? I call that the "booty triangle." Fold it over to create a clean, straight line.

4 Fold in half from bottom to top.

5 Place into a drawer with the rounded edge facing up.

Pants

1 Lay the pants faceup on a flat surface.

2 Fold in half from right to left.

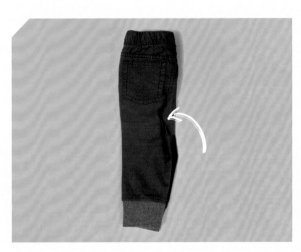

3 Notice the little triangle at the booty part of the pants? I call that the "booty triangle." Fold it over to create a clean, straight line.

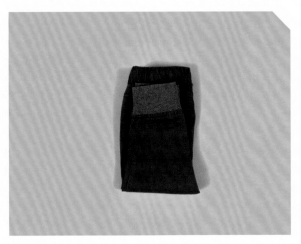

4 Fold up the legs to right below the waistline.

5 Fold in half from bottom to top.

6 Place into a drawer with the rounded edge facing up.

Leggings

1 Lay the leggings faceup on a flat surface.

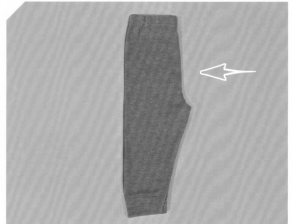

2 Fold in half from right to left.

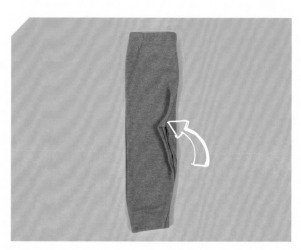

3 Notice the little triangle at the booty part of the leggings? I call that the "booty triangle." Fold it over to create a clean, straight line.

4 Fold up the legs to right below the waistline.

5 Fold in half from bottom to top.

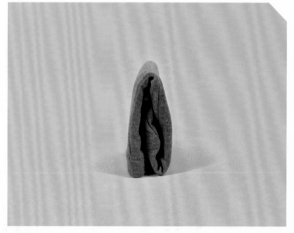

6 Place into a drawer with the rounded edge facing up.

Sweatpants

1 Lay the sweatpants faceup on a flat surface.

2 Fold in half from right to left. Notice the little triangle at the booty part of the sweatpants? I call that the "booty triangle." Fold it over to create a clean, straight line.

3 Fold up the legs to right below the waistline.

4 Fold in half from bottom to top.

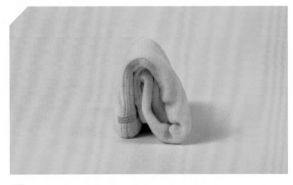

5 Place into a drawer with the rounded edge facing up.

Janelle says . . .

See page 126 to learn how to fold a sweat suit into a set.

Overalls

1 Lay the overalls facedown on a flat surface. Start with the overalls buttoned for easier folding.

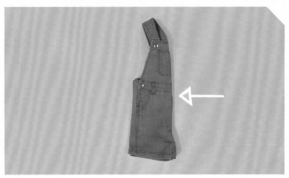

2 Fold in half from right to left.

3 Fold down the bib at the waist. Notice the little triangle at the booty part of the overalls? I call that the "booty triangle." Fold it over to create a clean, straight line.

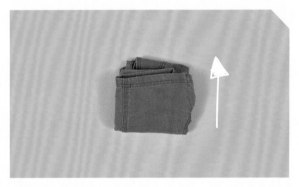

4 Fold in half from bottom to top.

5 Place into a drawer with the rounded edge facing up.

Janelle says . . .

If the overalls have long pants, in step 4, fold in half from bottom to top, and then fold in half again.

123

Dress

1 Lay the dress facedown on a flat surface.

2 Fold in the right side to the middle.

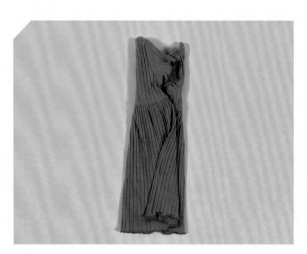

3 Fold the left side over the right side. If the bottom of the dress is wider at the bottom, fold it back toward the middle.

Janelle says . . . Dresses are ideally hung, but they can be folded to save space, especially if the fabric doesn't wrinkle easily.

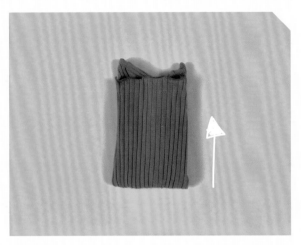

4 Bring up the bottom to right below the neckline.

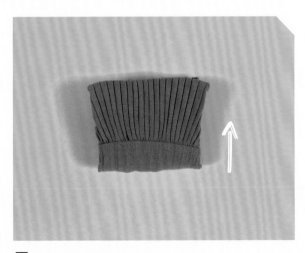

5 Fold in half from bottom to top.

6 Place into a drawer with the rounded edge facing up.

Sweat Suit

1 Starting with the sweatpants, lay them faceup on a flat surface.

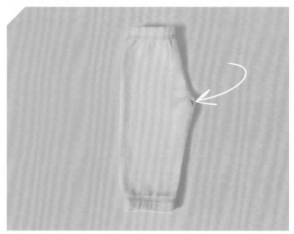

2 Fold in half from right to left. Notice the little triangle at the booty part of the sweatpants? I call that the "booty triangle." Fold it over to create a clean, straight line.

5 Moving on to the sweatshirt, lay it facedown on the flat surface.

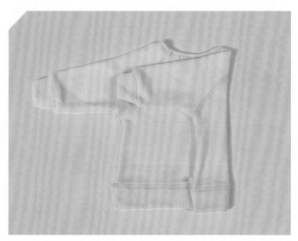

6 Fold in the right side slightly past the right edge of the neckline.

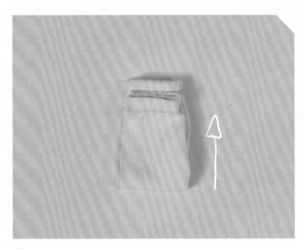

3 Fold up the legs to right below the waistline.

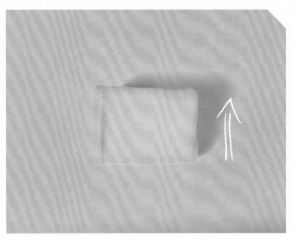

4 Fold in half from bottom to top. Set aside.

7 Fold the right sleeve back and down at the elbow so that it lies flat on the middle of the sweatshirt.

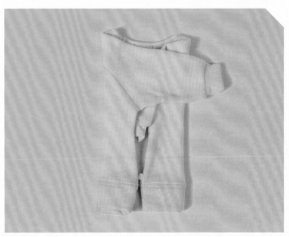

8 Fold in the left side to match the right side.

— — *Continued* — — ▷

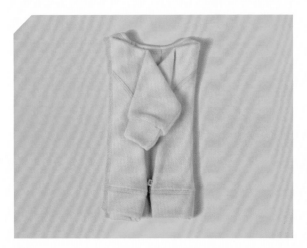

9 Fold the left sleeve back and down at the elbow and lay it on the right sleeve.

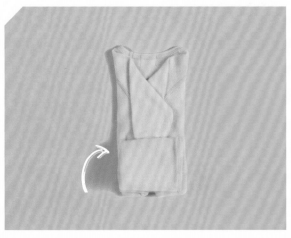

10 Place the folded sweatpants on the bottom of the sweatshirt.

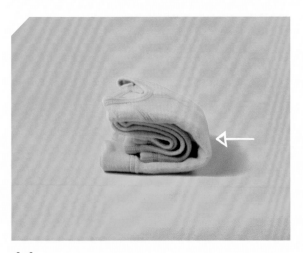

11 Fold in half from top to bottom, with the folded sweatpants tucked inside.

12 Place into a drawer with the rounded edge facing up.

Two-Piece Swimsuit

1 Starting with the swimsuit bottom, lay it faceup on a flat surface.

2 Fold in the right side to the middle.

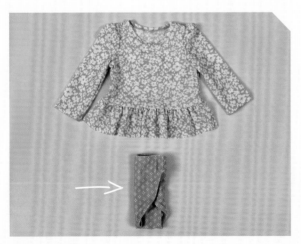

3 Fold the left side over the right side.

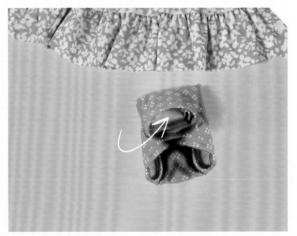

4 You have now created a pocket at the top.

– – Continued – –▷

5 Tuck the bottom section inside the pocket. Set aside.

6 Moving on to the swimsuit shirt, lay it facedown on the flat surface. Fold in the right side slightly past the right edge of the neckline.

9 Fold the left sleeve back, bend it down at the elbow, and lay it on top of the right sleeve.

10 Bring up the bottom of the top to the middle.

7 Fold the right sleeve back and bend it down at the elbow so that it lies flat on the middle of the shirt.

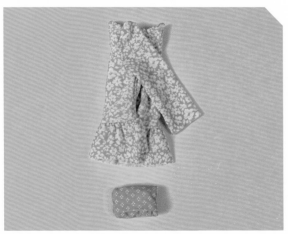

8 Fold in the left side to match the right side.

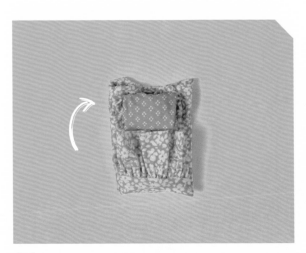

11 Place the folded bottom on the top half of the shirt.

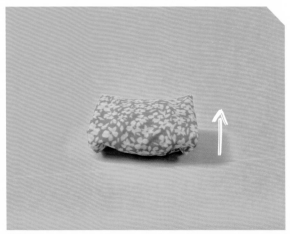

12 Fold in half from bottom to top, with the folded bottom tucked inside. Place into a drawer with the rounded edge facing up.

One-Piece Swimsuit

1 Lay the one-piece swimsuit faceup on a flat surface.

2 Fold in the right side slightly past the right edge of the neckline.

5 Fold the left sleeve back, bend it down at the elbow, and lay it on the right sleeve.

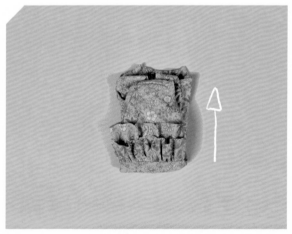

6 Bring up the bottom to right below the neckline.

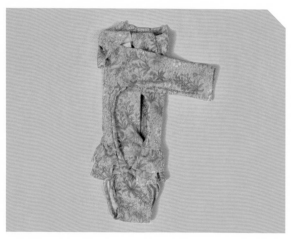

3 Fold the right sleeve back and bend it down at the elbow so that it lies flat on the middle of the swimsuit.

4 Fold in the left side to match the right side.

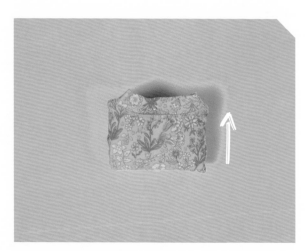

7 Fold in half from bottom to top. Place into a drawer with the rounded edge facing up.

Swim Trunks

1 Lay the swim trunks faceup on a flat surface.

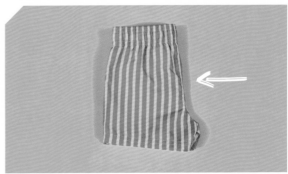

2 Fold in half from right to left.

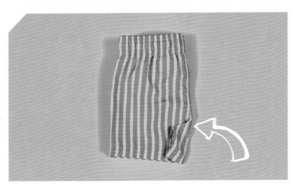

3 Notice the little triangle at the booty part of the swim trunks? I call that the "booty triangle." Fold it over to create a clean, straight line.

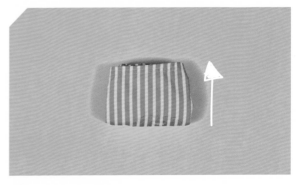

4 Fold in half from bottom to top.

5 Place into a drawer with the rounded edge facing up.

Socks

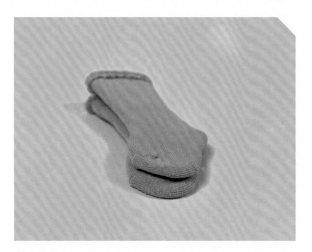

1 Lay the socks on top of each other on a flat surface.

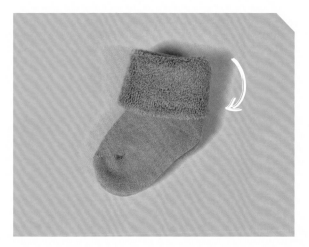

2 Turn down the top of one of the socks halfway over the pair to bundle them.

Janelle says . . . You can also use this folding method for keeping mittens together.

Beanie

1 Place the beanie on a flat surface.

2 Fold in half from right to left.

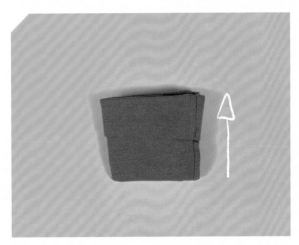

3 Fold in half from bottom to top. Place into a drawer with the rounded edge facing up.

Bib

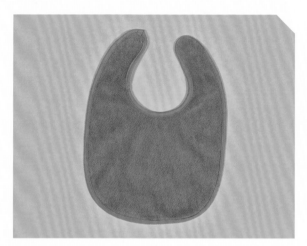

1 Lay the bib facedown on a flat surface.

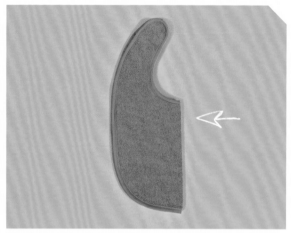

2 Fold in half from right to left.

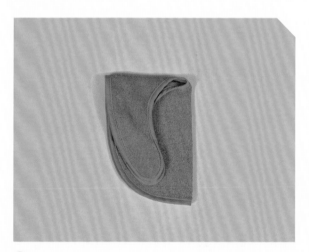

3 Fold down the top straps to create a straight line across the top.

4 Fold in half from bottom to top. Place into a drawer with the rounded edge facing up.

Bandana Bib

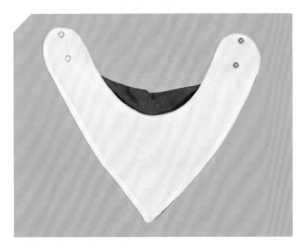

1 Lay the bandana bib facedown on a flat surface.

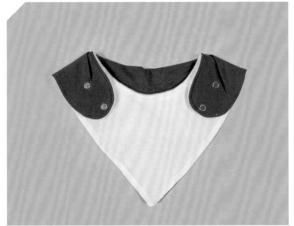

2 Fold down the flaps.

5 You have now created a pocket at the top.

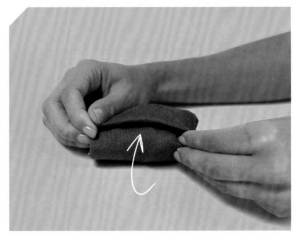

6 Tuck the bottom triangle inside the pocket.

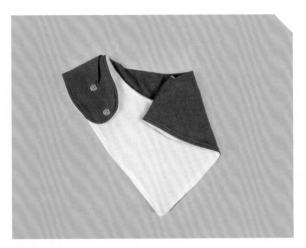

3 Fold in the right side to the middle.

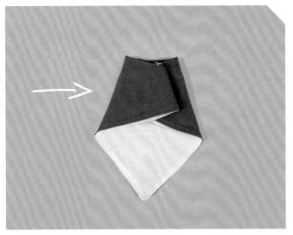

4 Fold the left side over the right side.

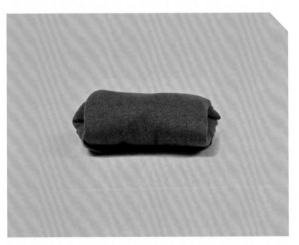

7 Place into a drawer with the round edge facing up.

Hooded Towel

1 Lay the hooded towel facedown on a flat surface.

2 Fold in the right side to the middle.

3 Fold the left side over the right side. If there is a hood, fold it down.

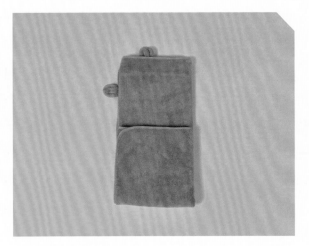

4 Flip over, if needed, so any sleeves or ears are facedown. Bring up the bottom to the middle.

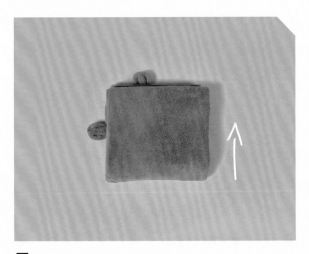

5 Fold up the bottom again and align at the top.

6 Place on a shelf with the rounded edge facing out.

Burp Cloth

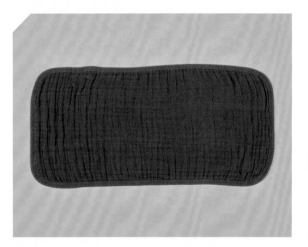

1 Lay the burp cloth horizontally on a flat surface.

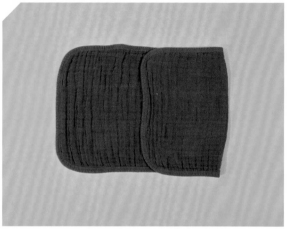

2 Fold in the right side to the middle.

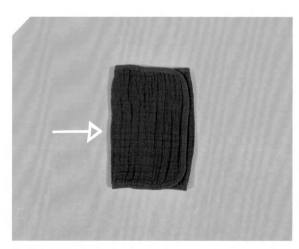

3 Fold the left side over the right side.

4 You should now have a pocket at the top.

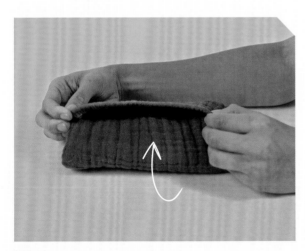

5 Tuck the bottom inside the pocket.

6 Place into a drawer with the pocket opening facing down.

Muslin Blanket

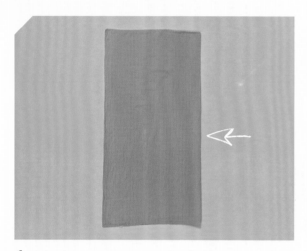

1 Lay the muslin blanket facedown on a flat surface. Fold in half from right to left.

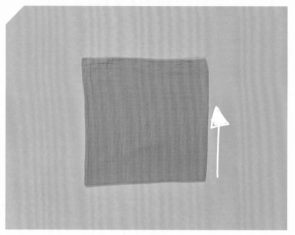

2 Fold in half from bottom to top.

5 Bring up the bottom to the middle.

6 Fold up the bottom again and align with the top.

3 Fold in the right side to the middle.

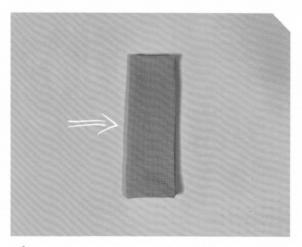

4 Fold the left side over the right side.

7 Place into a drawer with the rounded edge facing up or store on a shelf with the rounded edge facing out.

Sleep Sack

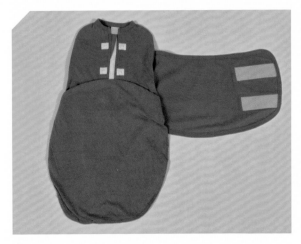

1 Lay the sleep sack faceup on a flat surface. If it has a zipper, zip it up so that it is easier to fold.

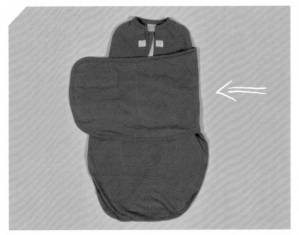

2 Fold the flap across the sleep sack.

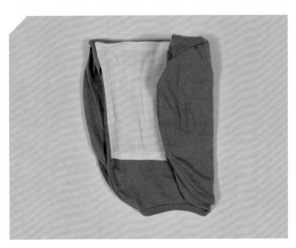

5 Fold in the right side to the middle.

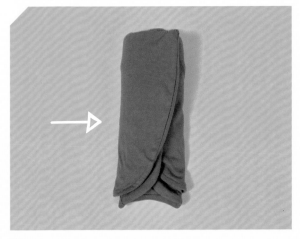

6 Fold the left side over the right side.

Janelle says...

Every sleep sack is structured a little differently, so adjust as needed.

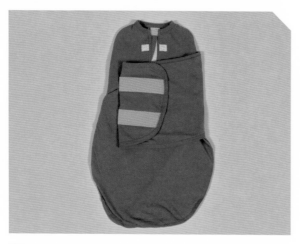

3 Fold back the flap to the middle of the sleep sack.

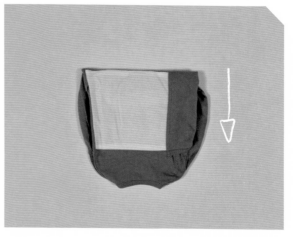

4 Fold the sleep sack in half from top to bottom.

7 Fold in half again, from bottom to top. Place into a drawer with the rounded edge facing up.

Crib Sheet

1 Turn the crib sheet inside out.

2 While standing, place each hand in a corner of one of the wide sides.

5 Switch your left hand with your right hand.

6 Slowly walk your hands down the sheet, one over the other inside the sheet. The sheet will naturally flip over and align as you move your hands down to the bottom corner.

3 Bring the right hand over to meet the left.

4 Flip the right corner over the left corner. Both sides should be together and being held by the left hand.

7 When you get to the bottom corner, flip it over to untangle.

8 When you have reached the bottom corner and flipped it over, it should look like a rectangle.

— — *Continued* — —▷

9 Lay the sheet on a flat surface. Clean up the edges and smooth out any wrinkles.

10 Fold in the right side to the middle.

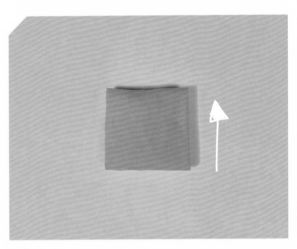

13 Fold up the bottom again and align with the top.

14 Place into a drawer with the rounded edge facing up or store on a shelf with the rounded edge facing out.

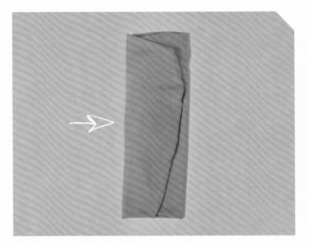

11 Fold the left side over the right side.

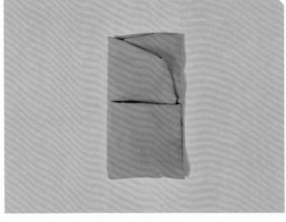

12 Bring up the bottom to the middle.

Janelle says... If you can master folding a crib sheet, then you're well on your way to succeeding at folding the dreaded Fitted Sheet on page 202!

Kid

Tank Top
154

Short-Sleeve T-Shirt
156, 157

Short-Sleeve Button-Down
158

Polo Shirt
159

Long-Sleeve T-Shirt
160

Cardigan
162

Hoodie
164

Athletic Shorts
166

Shorts
168

Pants
169

Dress
170

Skirt
172

Sweat Suit
174

Pajama Set
177

One-Piece Swimsuit
180

Two-Piece Swimsuit
182

Swim Trunks
184

Ankle Socks
185

Underwear
186

Boxer Briefs
188

Tank Top

1 Lay the tank top facedown on a flat surface.

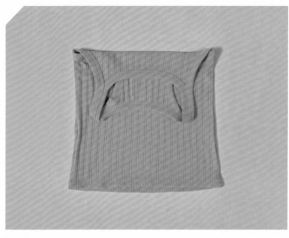

2 Fold down the straps at the base of the armpits to create a straight line across the top.

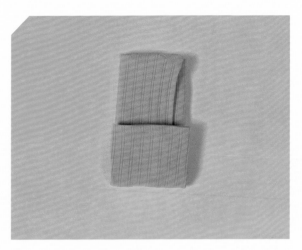

5 Bring up the bottom to the middle.

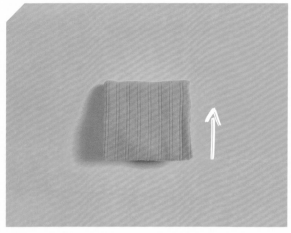

6 Fold up the bottom again and align with the top.

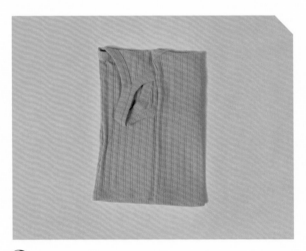

3 Fold in the right side to the middle.

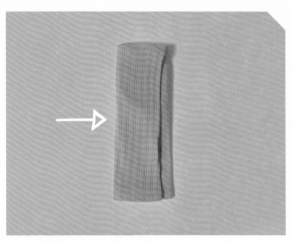

4 Fold the left side over the right side.

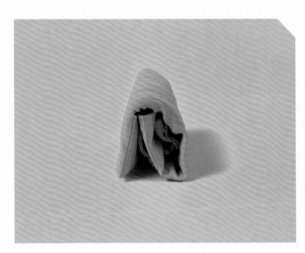

7 Place into a drawer with the rounded edge facing up.

Short-Sleeve T-Shirt

1 Lay the short-sleeve T-shirt facedown on a flat surface.

2 Fold in the right side slightly past the right edge of the neckline. Fold in the left side to match the right side.

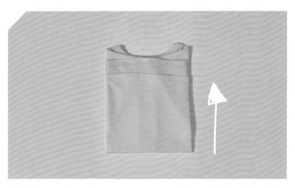

3 Bring up the bottom to right below the neckline.

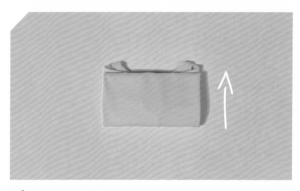

4 Fold in half from bottom to top.

5 Place into a drawer with the rounded edge facing up.

Janelle says . . .

If the shirt has a graphic on it, the graphic side should be facedown in step 1. This way you will see the identifying graphic when it is file-folded in the drawer.

Short-Sleeve T-Shirt (Variation)

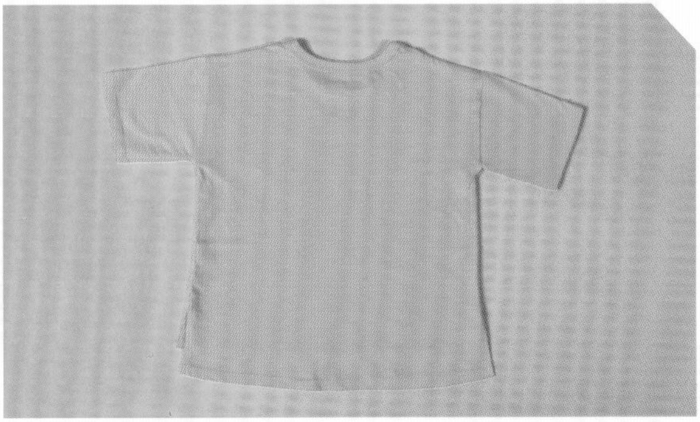

1 Lay the short-sleeve T-shirt facedown on a flat surface.

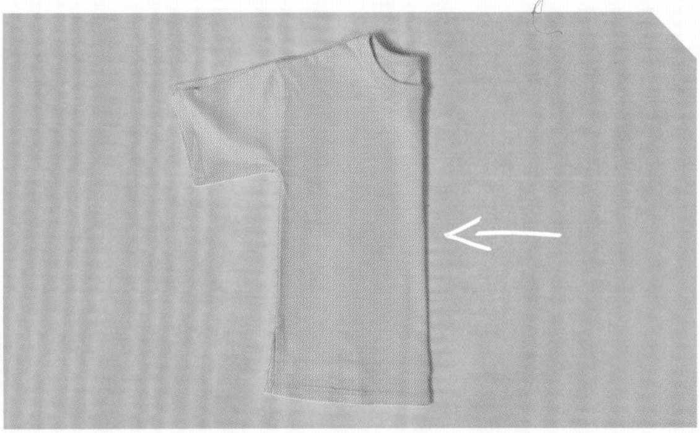

2 Fold in half from right to left.

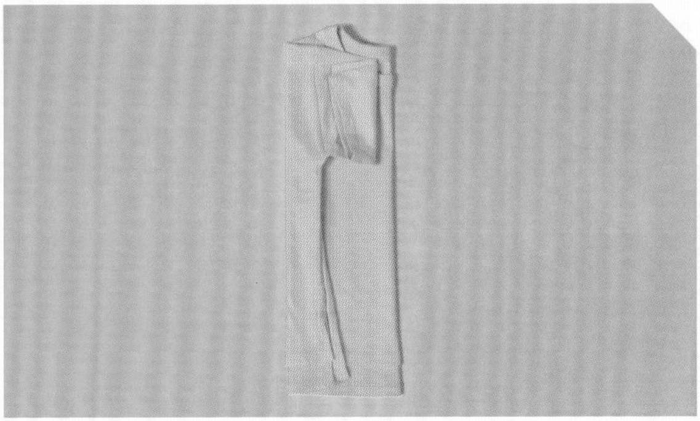

3 Fold the left side inward toward the right side. Fold back the sleeves if they overcross the right side.

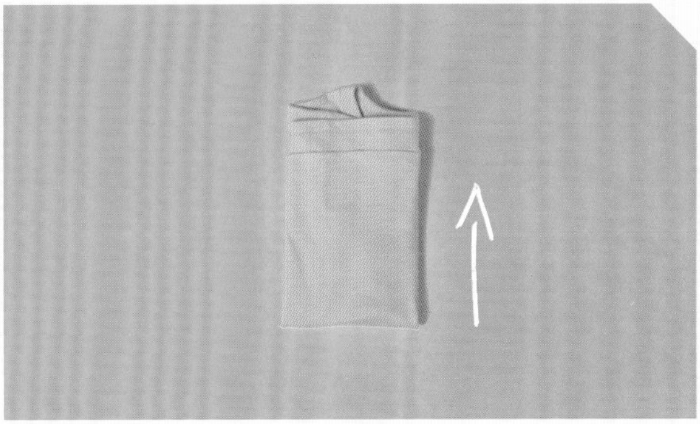

4 Bring up the bottom to right below the neckline.

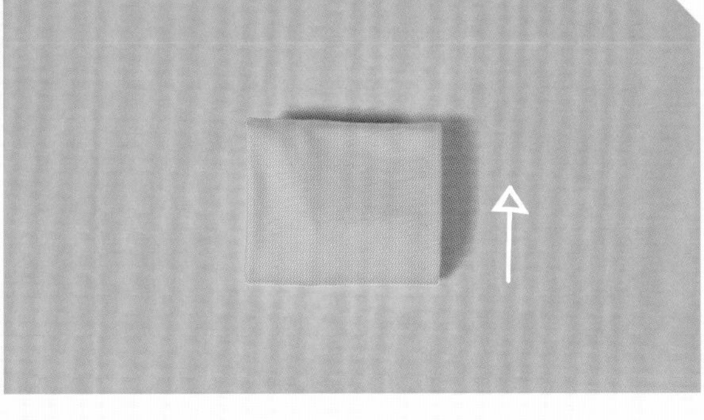

5 Fold in half from bottom to top.

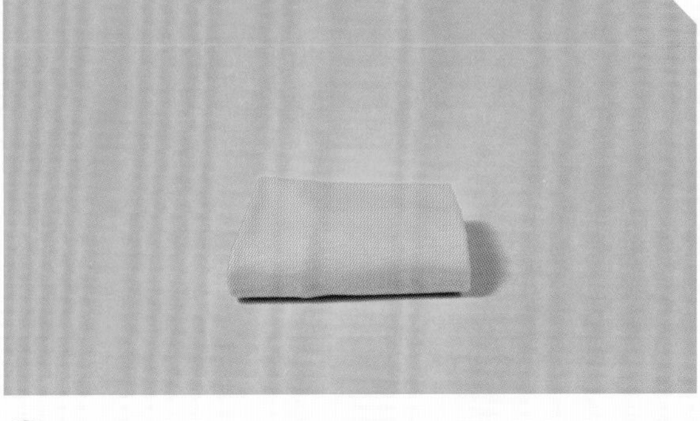

6 Place into a drawer with the rounded edge facing up.

Short-Sleeve Button-Down

1 Lay the short-sleeve button-down facedown on a flat surface.

2 Fold in the right side toward the middle.

3 Fold in the left side to match the right side.

4 Bring up the bottom up to right below the collar.

5 To avoid damaging the collar, place on a shelf faceup with the rounded edge facing out.

Janelle says . . .

The shirt will be easier to fold if it is buttoned. You can button all the buttons, or just the top, middle, and bottom buttons.

Polo Shirt

1 Lay the polo shirt facedown on a flat surface.

2 Fold in the right side toward the middle.

3 Fold in the left side to match the right side.

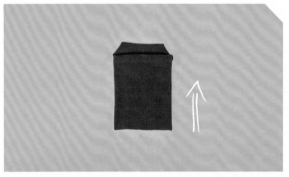

4 Bring up the bottom to right below the collar.

5 To avoid damaging the collar, place on a shelf faceup with the rounded edge facing out.

Janelle says . . .

The shirt will be easier to fold if it is buttoned, or you can just button the top button.

Long-Sleeve T-Shirt

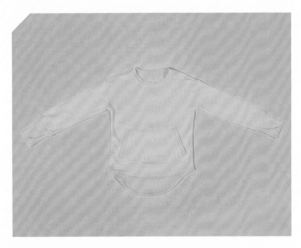

1 Lay the long-sleeve T-shirt facedown on a flat surface.

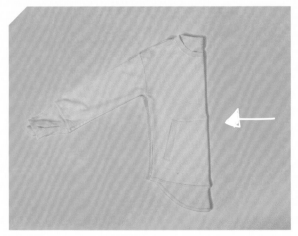

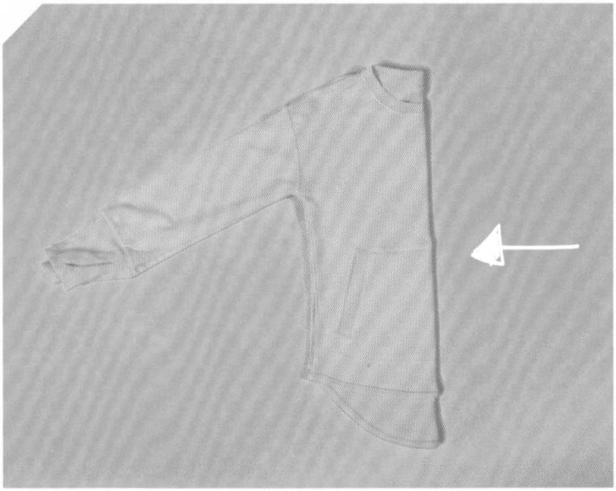

2 Fold in half from right to left.

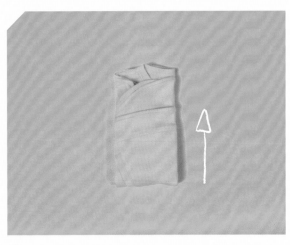

5 Bring up the bottom to right below the neckline.

6 Fold in half from bottom to top.

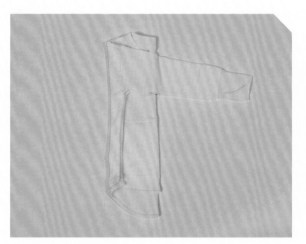

3 Fold the left side inward toward the right side.

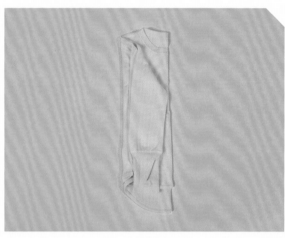

4 Fold the sleeves back and bend them down at the elbow so that they lie flat on the middle of the shirt.

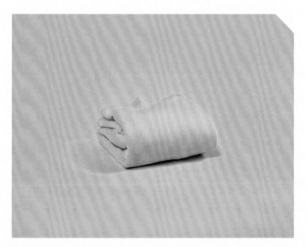

7 Place into a drawer with the rounded edge facing up.

Janelle says . . .

If the shirt has a graphic on it, the graphic side should be facedown in step 1. This way you will see the identifying graphic when it is file-folded in the drawer.

Cardigan

1 Lay the cardigan facedown on a flat surface with all the buttons buttoned.

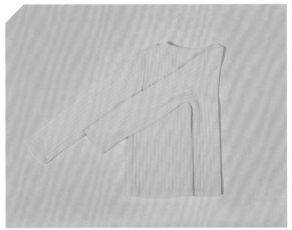

2 Fold in the right side slightly past the right edge of the neckline.

5 Fold the left sleeve back, bend it down at the elbow, and lay it on top of the right sleeve.

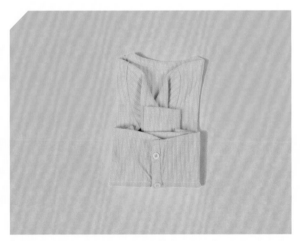

6 Bring up the bottom to the middle.

Janelle says... You can use this folding method for all sweater styles. If storing on a shelf, in step 6, fold up the bottom to right below the neckline and place faceup on the shelf with the rounded edge facing out.

3 Fold the right sleeve back and bend it down at the elbow so that it lies flat on the middle of the sweater.

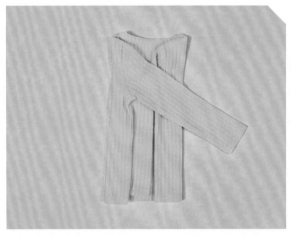

4 Fold in the left side to match the right side.

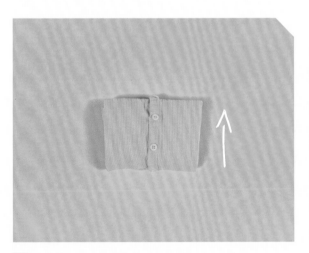

7 Fold up the bottom again and align with the top.

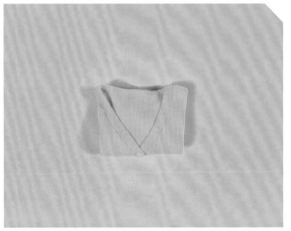

8 Place into a drawer with the rounded edge facing up. If storing on a shelf, see the tip at the top of the page.

Hoodie

1 Lay the hoodie facedown on a flat surface. Make sure the hood is flat.

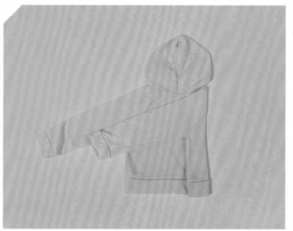

2 Fold in the right side slightly past the right edge of the hood.

5 Fold the left sleeve back, bend it down at the elbow, and lay it on top of the right sleeve.

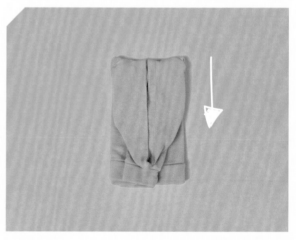

6 Fold down the hood and lay any strings on the hood.

Janelle says... If the hoodie has a zipper, zip it up to make folding easier.

3 Fold the right sleeve back and bend it down at the elbow so that it lies flat on the hoodie.

4 Fold in the left side to match the right side.

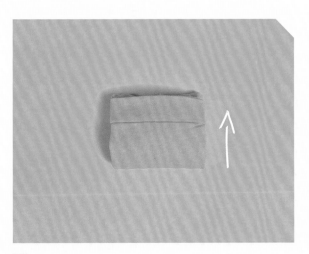

7 Fold the sweatshirt in half from bottom to top.

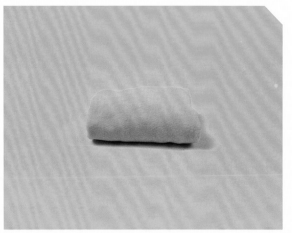

8 Place into a drawer with the rounded edge facing up or store on a shelf with the rounded edge facing out.

Athletic Shorts

1 Lay the athletic shorts faceup on a flat surface.

2 Fold in the right side to the middle.

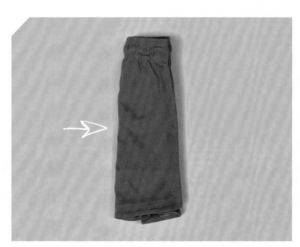

3 Fold the left side over the right side.

Janelle says... Because athletic shorts are often made of a slinky fabric, this tucked fold works better at keeping them folded than a regular fold.

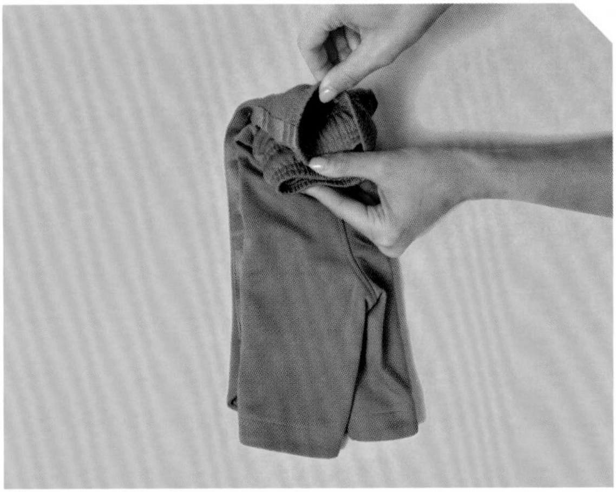

4 Flip the shorts over. (Trust me; it helps.) You have now created a pocket at the top.

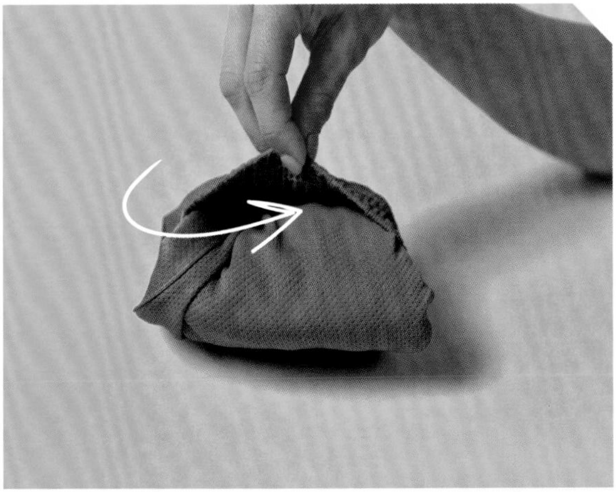

5 Tuck the bottom inside the pocket.

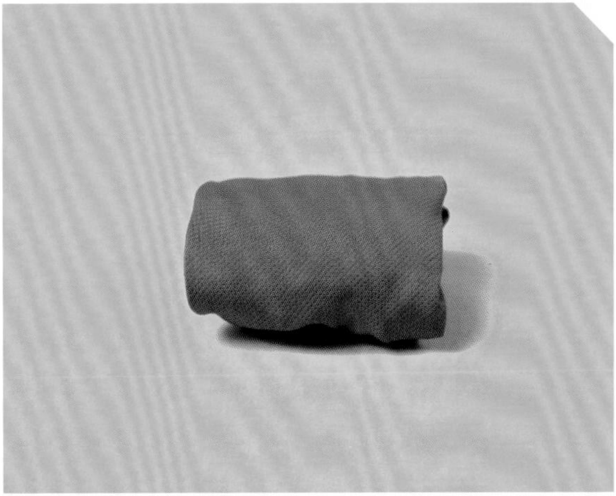

6 Place into a drawer with the pocket opening facing down.

Shorts

1 Lay the shorts faceup on a flat surface.

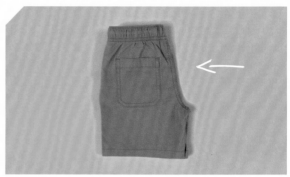

2 Fold in half from right to left.

3 Notice the little triangle at the booty part of the shorts? I call that the "booty triangle." Fold it over to create a clean, straight line.

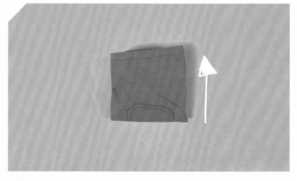

4 Bring up the bottom to right below the waistline.

5 Place into a drawer with the rounded edge facing up.

Pants

1 Lay the pants faceup on a flat surface.

2 Fold in half from right to left. Notice the little triangle at the booty part of the pants? I call that the "booty triangle." Fold it over to create a clean, straight line.

3 Bring up the legs to right below the waistline.

4 Fold in half from bottom to top.

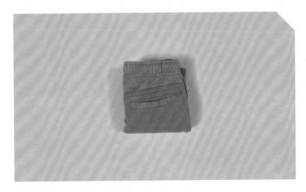

5 Place into a drawer with the rounded edge facing up.

Dress

1 Lay the dress facedown on a flat surface.

2 Fold in the right side to the middle. If the dress is wider at the bottom, fold it back toward the right side.

5 Fold in half from bottom to top.

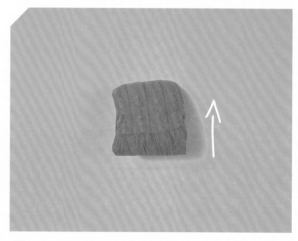

6 Fold in half again, from bottom to top.

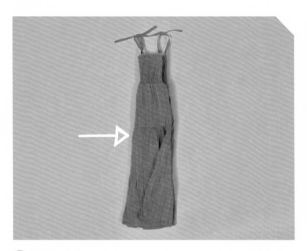

3 Fold the left side over the right side. If the dress is wider at the bottom, fold it back toward the middle.

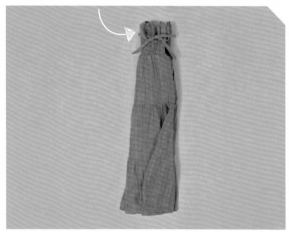

4 Fold down the straps.

7 Place into a drawer with the rounded edge facing up.

Janelle says . . .

Dresses are ideally hung, but they can be folded to save space, especially if the fabric doesn't wrinkle easily.

Skirt

1 Lay the skirt faceup on a flat surface.

2 Fold in the right side to the middle.

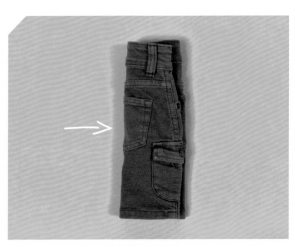

3 Fold the left side over the right side.

Janelle says... If the skirt is too small to fold into thirds, just fold it in half.

4 Bring up the bottom to the middle.

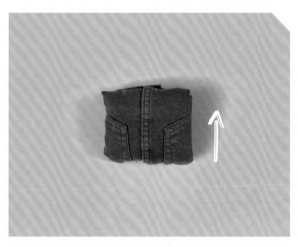

5 Fold up the bottom again and align with the top.

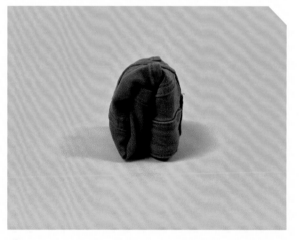

6 Place into a drawer with the rounded edge facing up.

Sweat Suit

1 Starting with the sweatpants, lay them faceup on a flat surface.

2 Fold in half from right to left.

5 Fold in half from bottom to top. Set aside.

6 Moving on to the sweatshirt, lay it facedown on the flat surface.

3 Notice the little triangle at the booty part of the sweatpants? I call that the "booty triangle." Fold it over to create a clean, straight line.

4 Bring up the legs to right below the waistline.

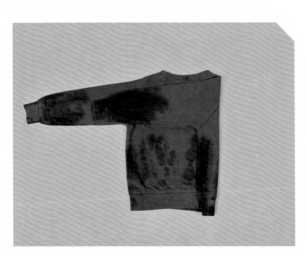

7 Fold in the right side slightly past the right side of the neckline.

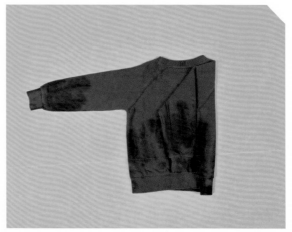

8 Fold the right sleeve back and bend it down at the elbow so that it lies flat on the middle of the sweatshirt.

— — *Continued* — —▷

9 Fold in the left side to match the right side.

10 Fold the left sleeve back, bend it down at the elbow, and lay it on top of the right sleeve.

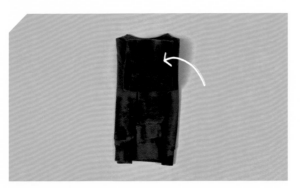

11 Place the folded sweatpants on the sweatshirt right below the neckline.

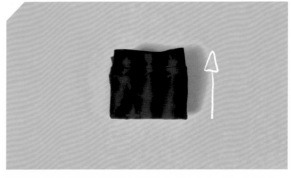

12 Fold in half from bottom to top, with the folded sweatpants tucked inside.

13 Place into a drawer with the rounded edge facing up or store on a shelf with the rounded edge facing out.

Pajama Set

1 Starting with the pajama bottoms, lay them faceup on a flat surface.

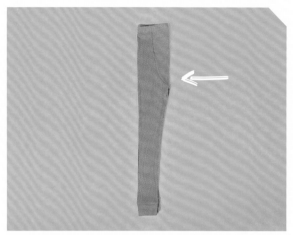

2 Fold in half from right to left.

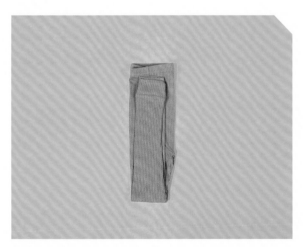

3 Fold up the legs to right below the waistline.

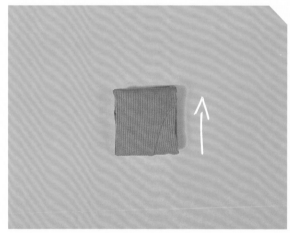

4 Fold in thirds by bringing up the bottom to the middle, and then folding up the bottom again and aligning with the top. Set aside.

- - - *Continued* - -▷

5 Moving on to the pajama shirt, lay it facedown on the flat surface.

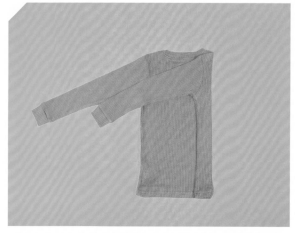

6 Fold in the right side slightly past the right edge of the neckline.

9 Fold the left sleeve back, bend it down at the elbow, and lay it on top of the right sleeve.

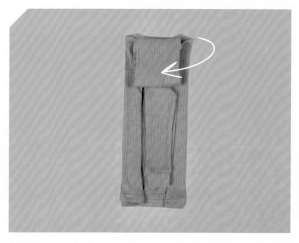

10 Place the folded bottoms on the top of the shirt right below the neckline.

Janelle says . . . Keep pajama sets folded together in the drawer to make it easier for kids to get ready for bed by themselves!

7 Fold the right sleeve back and bend it down at the elbow so that it lies flat on the middle of the top.

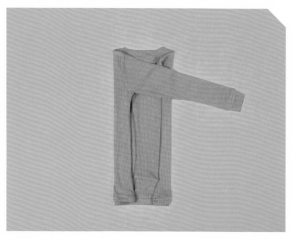

8 Fold in the left side to match the right side.

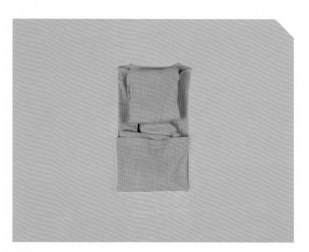

11 Bring up the bottom of the shirt to the middle.

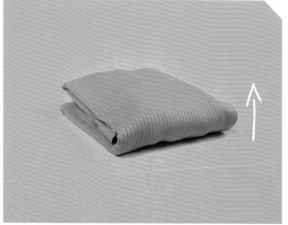

12 Fold up the bottom of the shirt again and align with the top, with the pants tucked inside. Place into a drawer with the rounded edge facing up.

One-Piece Swimsuit

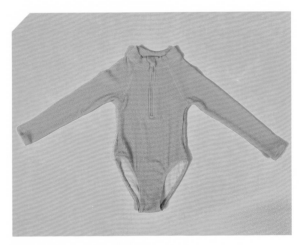

1 Lay the one-piece swimsuit faceup on a flat surface.

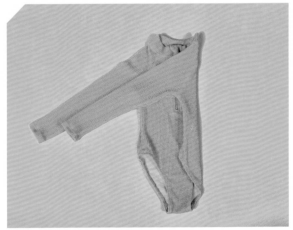

2 Fold in the right side slightly past the right edge of the neckline.

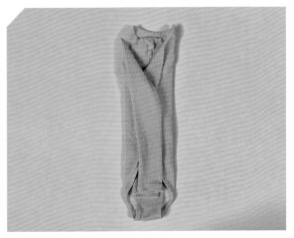

5 Fold the left sleeve back, bend it down at the elbow, and lay it on top of the right sleeve.

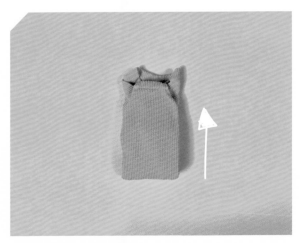

6 Bring up the bottom to right below the neckline.

3 Fold the right sleeve back and bend it down at the elbow so that it lies flat on the middle of the swimsuit.

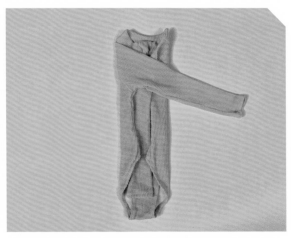

4 Fold in the left side to match the right side.

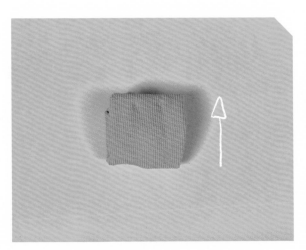

7 Fold in half from bottom to top.

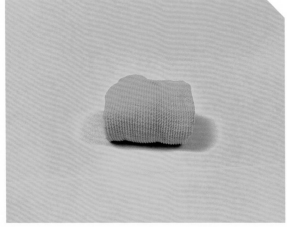

8 Place into a drawer with the rounded edge facing up.

Two-Piece Swimsuit

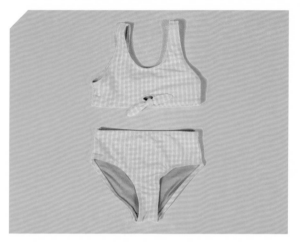

1 Starting with the swimsuit bottom, lay it faceup on a flat surface.

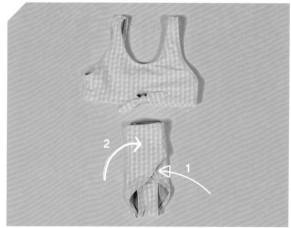

2 Fold in the right side to the middle, and then fold the left side over the right side.

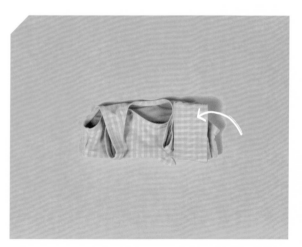

5 Place the folded bottom vertically on the right side of the top.

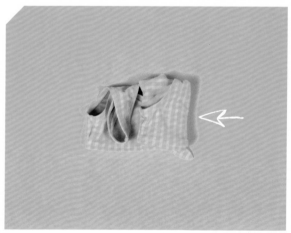

6 Fold over the right side to the middle, with the folded bottoms tucked inside.

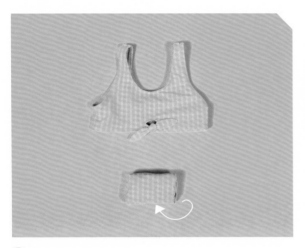

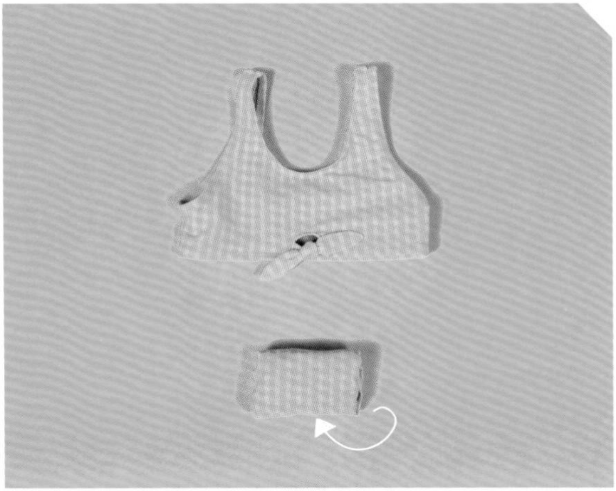

3 There is now a pocket at the top (see step 4 photo on page 187 for a visual). Tuck the bottom section inside the pocket. Set aside.

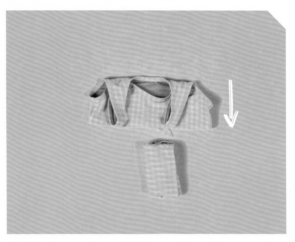

4 Moving on to the swimsuit top, lay it facedown on a flat surface. Fold down the straps to the bottom of the top.

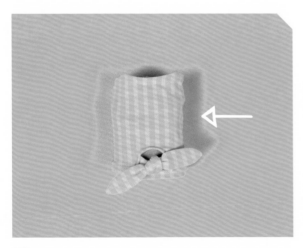

7 Fold over the right side again and align with the left side.

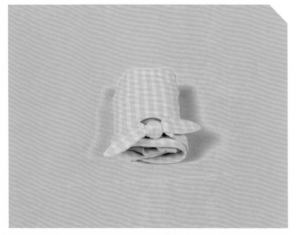

8 Place into a drawer with the rounded edge facing up.

Swim Trunks

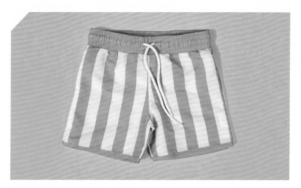

1 Lay the swim trunks faceup on a flat surface.

2 Fold in half from right to left.

3 Bring up the bottom to the middle.

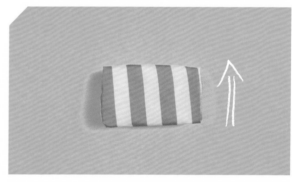

4 Fold up the bottom again and align with the top.

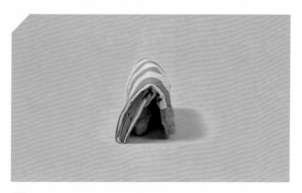

5 Place into a drawer with the rounded edge facing up.

Ankle Socks

1 Lay the socks on a flat surface with the tops of the socks facing up.

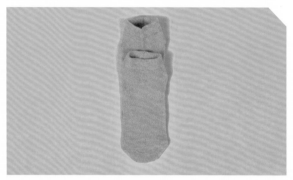

2 Place one sock on top of the other with the top sock below the ankle of the bottom sock.

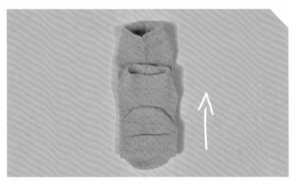

3 Fold up the top sock until it aligns with the toe of the bottom sock.

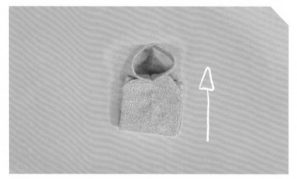

4 Fold up the bottom sock over the top sock.

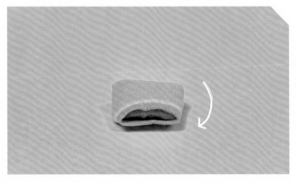

5 Turn down the opening of the bottom sock and wrap it around the folded parts to create a bundle.

Underwear

1 Lay the underwear faceup on a flat surface.

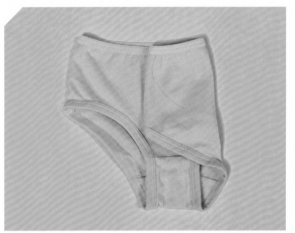

2 Fold in the right side to the middle.

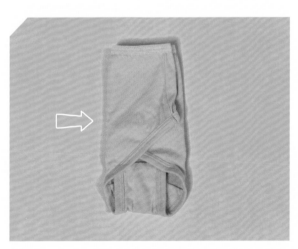

3 Fold the left side over the right side.

4 There is now a pocket at the top.

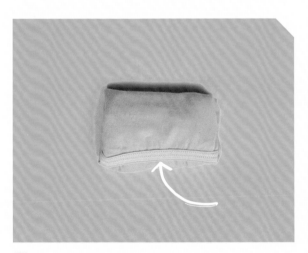

5 Tuck the bottom section inside the pocket.

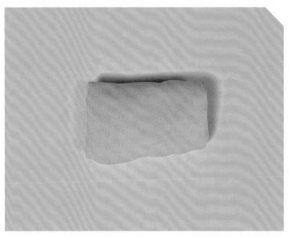

6 Place into a drawer with the pocket opening facing down.

Boxer Briefs

1 Lay the boxer briefs faceup on a flat surface.

2 Fold in the right side to the middle.

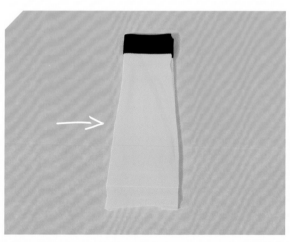

3 Fold the left side over the right side.

4 Flip the boxers over. (Trust me; it helps.) You have now created a pocket at the top.

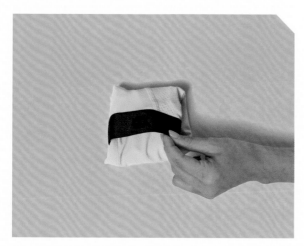

5 Tuck the legs inside the pocket.

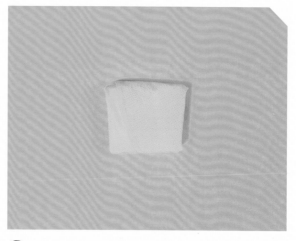

6 Place into a drawer with the pocket opening facing down.

Linens

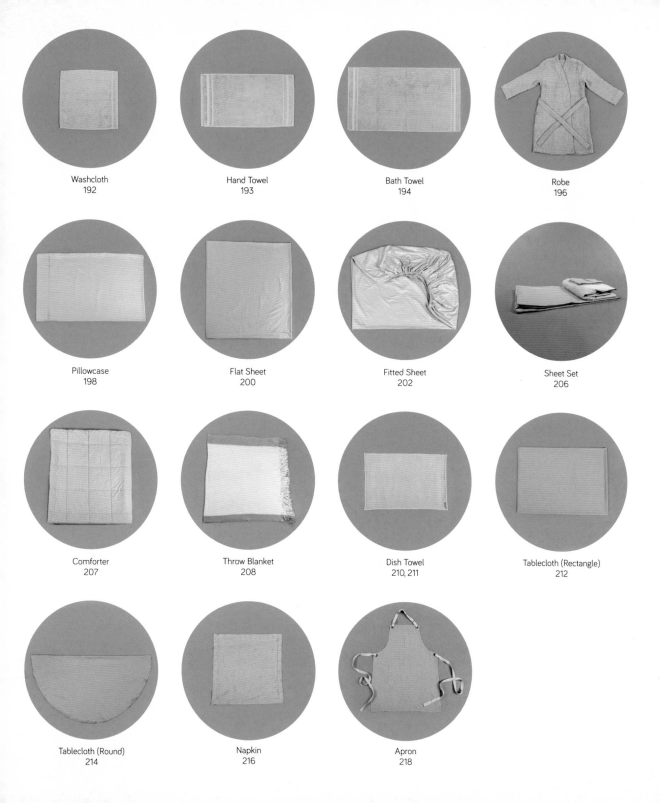

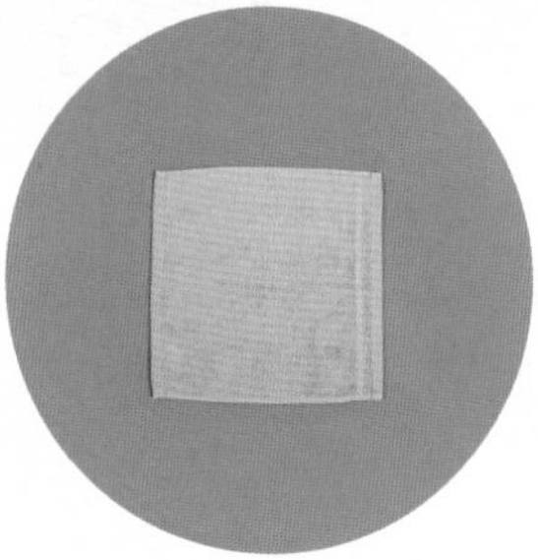
Washcloth
192

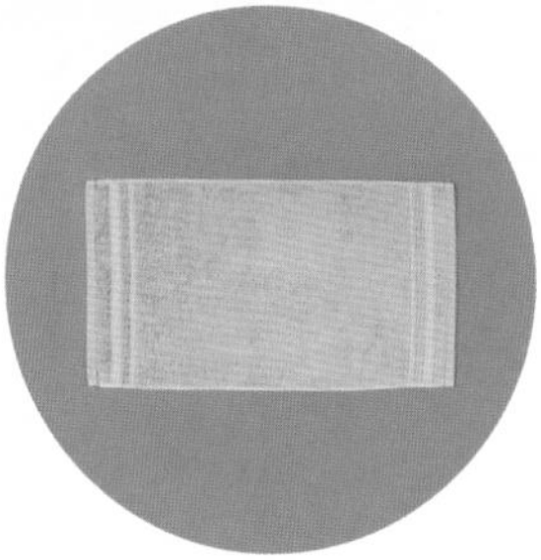
Hand Towel
193

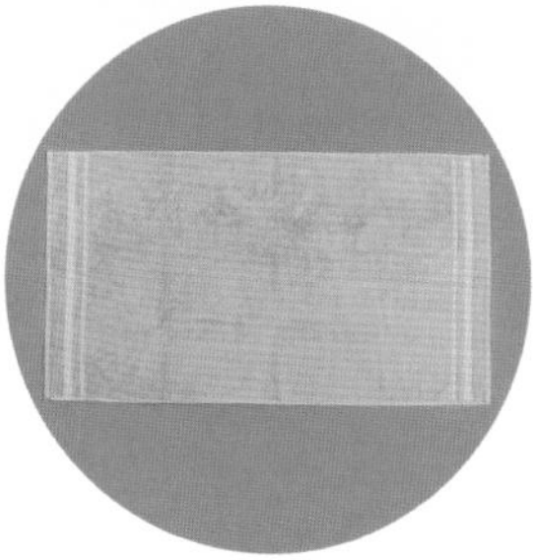
Bath Towel
194

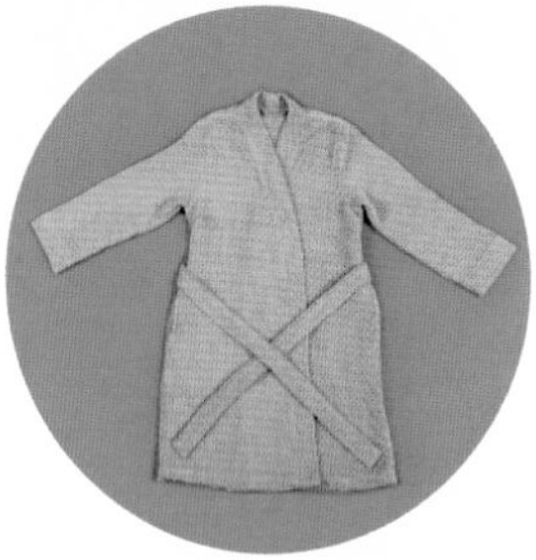
Robe
196

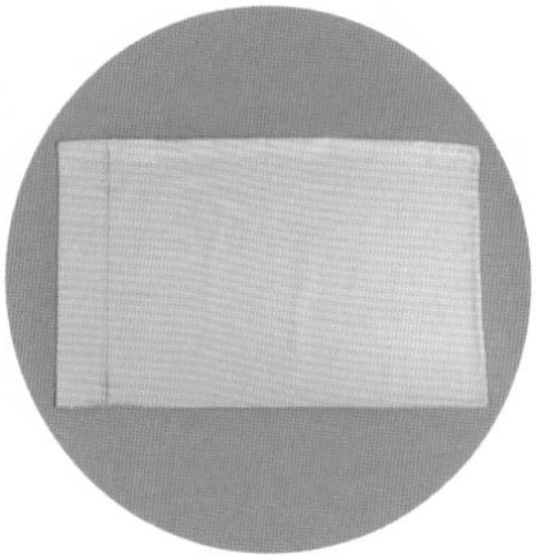
Pillowcase
198

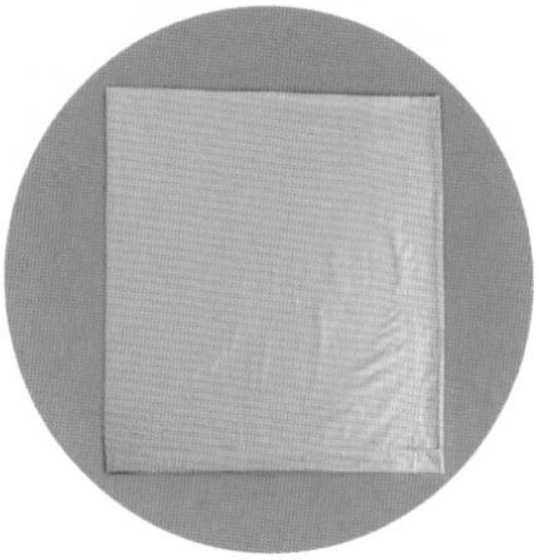
Flat Sheet
200

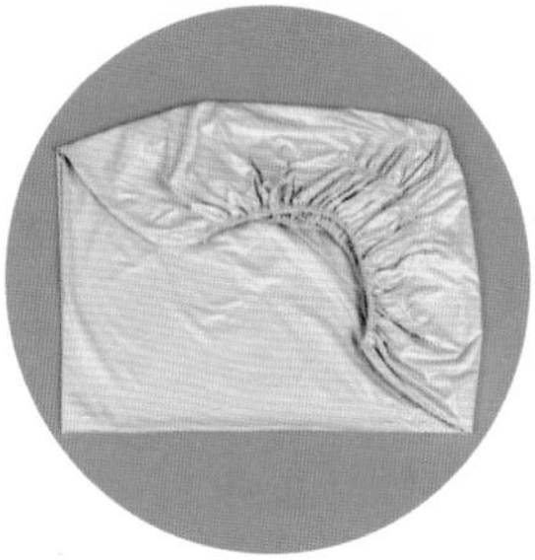
Fitted Sheet
202

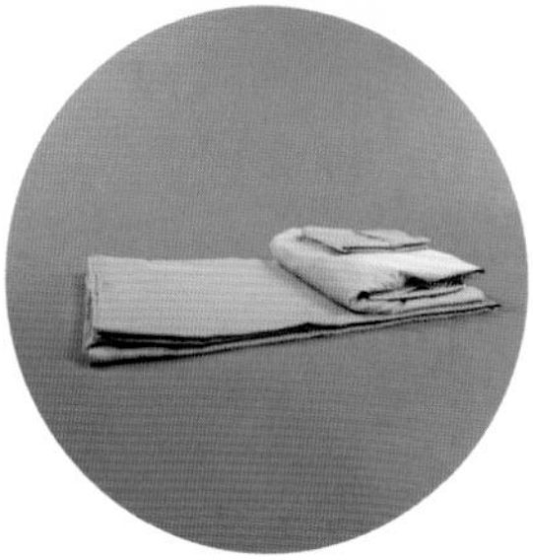
Sheet Set
206

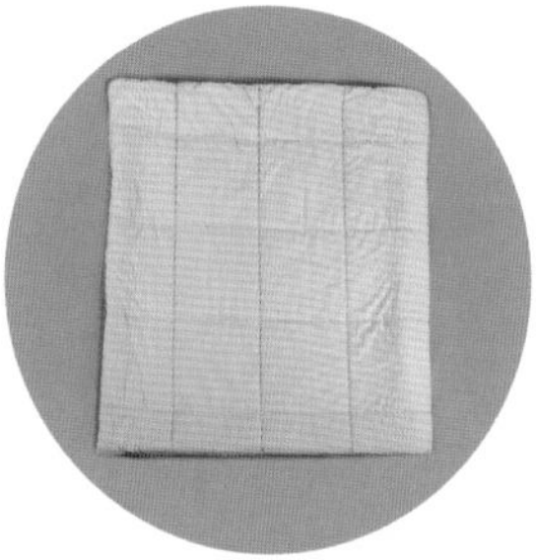
Comforter
207

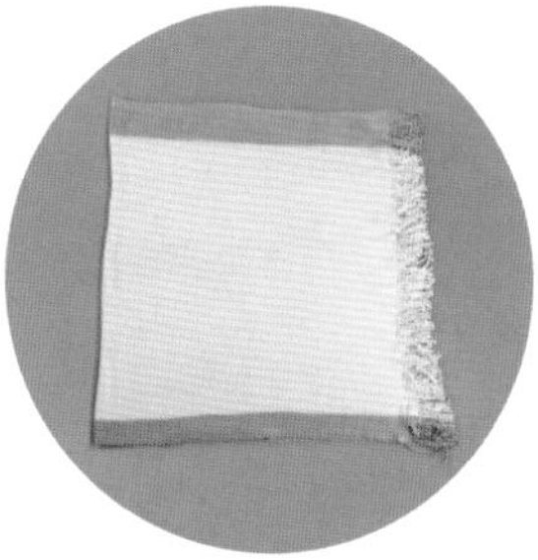
Throw Blanket
208

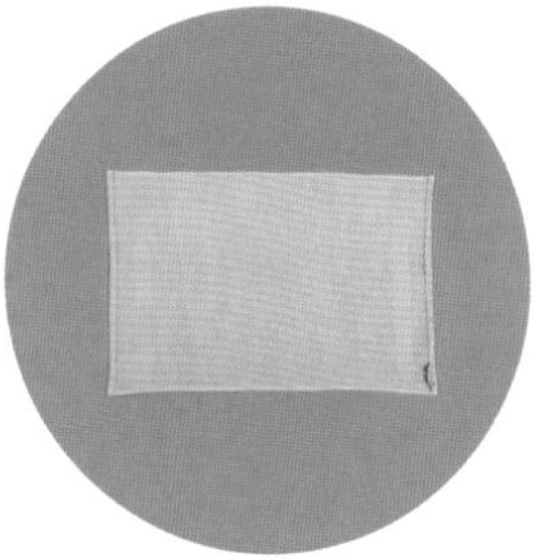
Dish Towel
210, 211

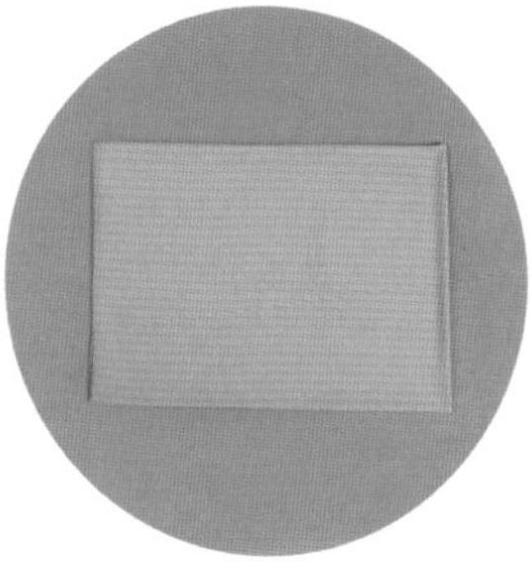
Tablecloth (Rectangle)
212

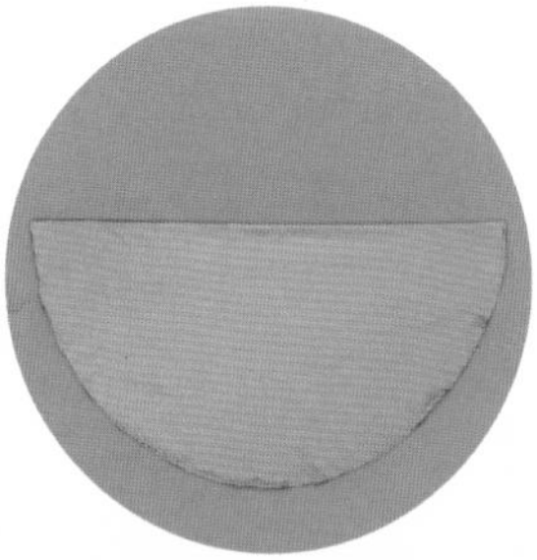
Tablecloth (Round)
214

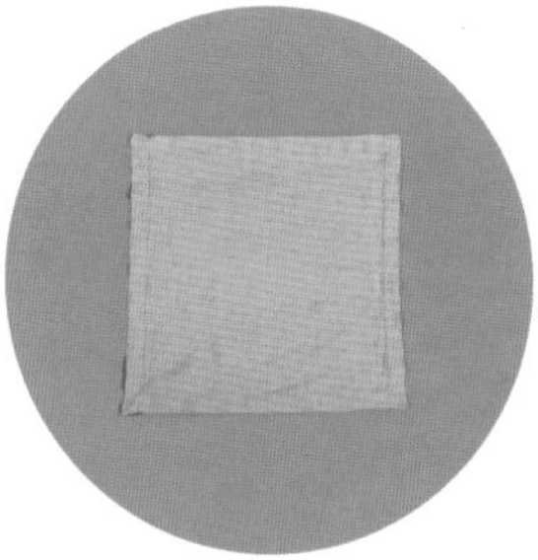
Napkin
216

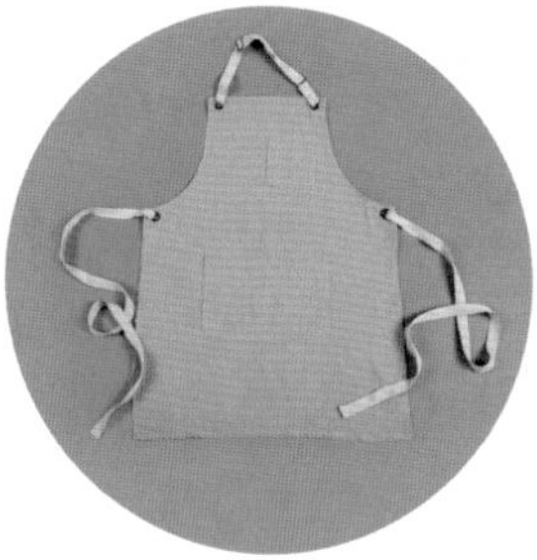
Apron
218

Washcloth

1 Lay the washcloth facedown on a flat surface.

2 Fold in half from left to right.

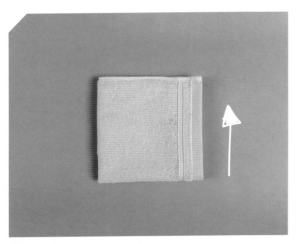

3 Fold in half again, from bottom to top.

4 Store on a shelf with the rounded edge facing out.

Hand Towel

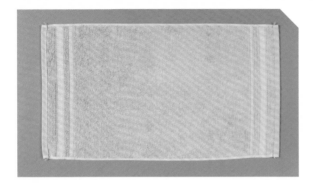

1 Lay the hand towel facedown horizontally on a flat surface.

2 Fold in half from left to right.

3 Fold down the top to the middle.

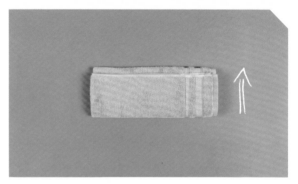

4 Fold up the bottom over the top.

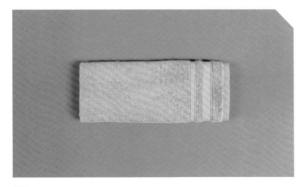

5 Flip it over and store on a shelf.

Bath Towel

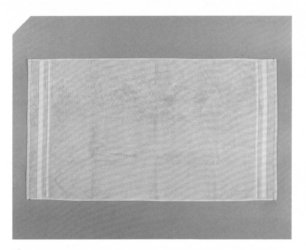

1 Lay the bath towel facedown horizontally on a flat surface.

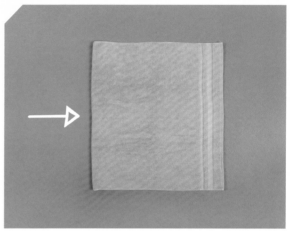

2 Fold in half from left to right.

3 Bring down the top to the middle.

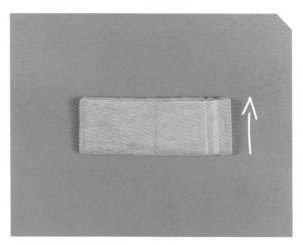

4 Fold up the bottom over the top.

5 Fold in half from right to left.

6 Store on a shelf with the rounded edge facing out.

Robe

1 Lay the robe faceup on a flat surface with the belt ends neatly crossed over each other on top of the robe.

2 Fold in the right side toward the middle.

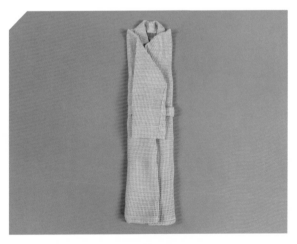

5 Fold the left sleeve back, bend it down at the elbow, and lay it on top of the right sleeve.

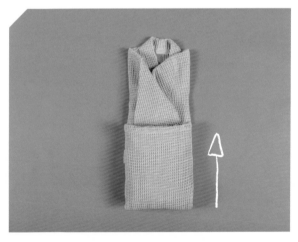

6 Bring up the bottom to the middle.

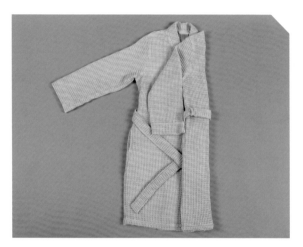

3 Fold the right sleeve back and bend it down at the elbow so that it lies flat on the middle of the robe.

4 Fold the left side over the right sleeve.

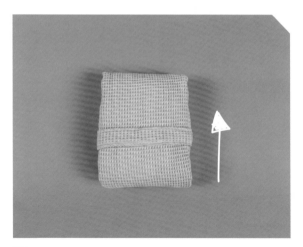

7 Fold up the bottom again and align with the top.

8 Store on a shelf with the rounded edge facing out.

Pillowcase

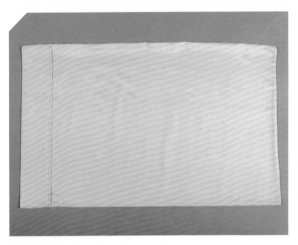

1 Lay the pillowcase horizontally on a flat surface.

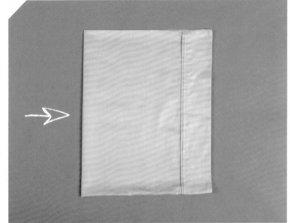

2 Fold in half from left to right.

3 Flip over the pillowcase so that the trim is facedown.

Janelle says... Pillow shams can be folded using this same method.

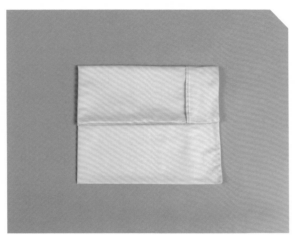

4 Bring down the top to the middle.

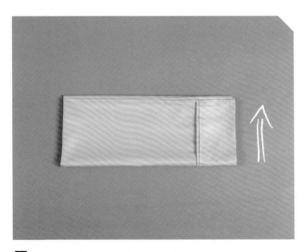

5 Fold up the bottom over the top.

6 Fold in half from right to left. If the pillowcase has trim, flip it over so that the trim is on top. Store on a shelf with the rounded edge facing out.

Flat Sheet

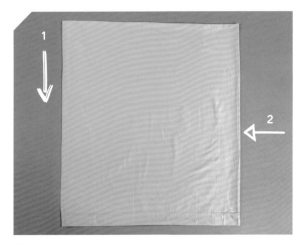

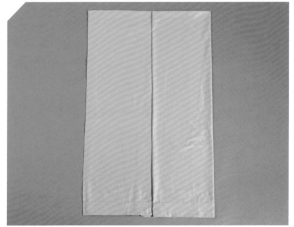

1 Lay the flat sheet horizontally on a flat surface. Fold in half from top to bottom, and then fold in half from right to left.

2 Fold in the right side to the middle.

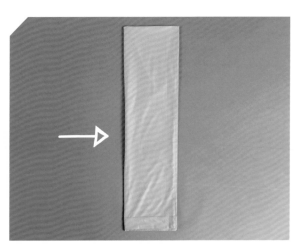

3 Fold the left side over the right side.

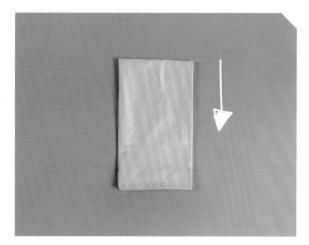

4 Fold in half from top to bottom.

5 Fold in half again, from top to bottom.

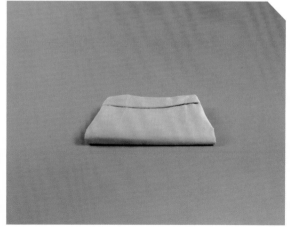

6 If the sheet has trim, flip it over so that trim is on top. Store on a shelf with the rounded edge facing out.

Fitted Sheet

1 Turn the fitted sheet inside out. While standing, place each hand in a corner of one of the wide sides.

2 Bring the right hand over to meet the left.

5 Switch your left hand with your right hand.

6 Slowly walk your hands down the sheet, one over the other inside the sheet. The sheet will naturally flip over and align as you move your hands down to the bottom corner.

3 Hold both corners with your left hand and pull out your right hand.

4 Flip the right corner over the left corner. Both sides should now be together and being held by the left hand.

7 When the sheet has been completely flipped over and untangled, repeat the process. Place each hand in a corner of one of the wide sides.

8 Bring the right hand over to meet the left. Hold both corners with your left hand and pull out your right hand.

– – Continued – –▷

9 Flip the right corner over the left corner. Both sides should now be together and being held by the left hand.

10 Slowly walk your hands down the sheet, flipping it over until you get to the farthest corner. When you get to the bottom corner, flip it over to untangle.

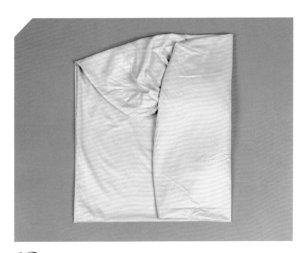

13 Fold in the right side to the middle.

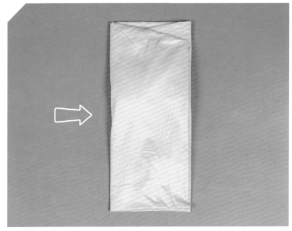

14 Fold the left side over the right side.

Don't expect to get this on the first try; it takes a little bit of practice. Mess around with it and figure out what works for you. And if you give up, no one is going to judge you for crumpling up the sheet and throwing it in the closet.

11 You should have created an "L" shape.

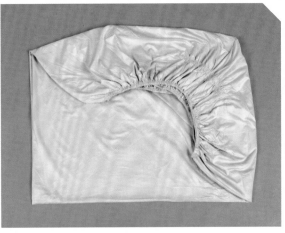

12 Lay your sheet on a flat surface. It should look like a rectangle. Clean up the edges and smooth out any wrinkles.

15 Bring up the bottom to the middle.

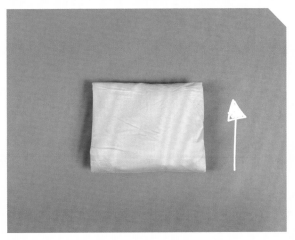

16 Fold up the bottom again and align with the top. Store on a shelf with the rounded edge facing out.

Sheet Set

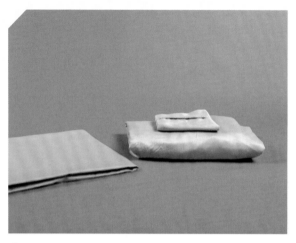

1 To fold a pillowcase(s), fitted sheet, and flat sheet into a sheet set, complete the folding of the pillowcase(s) (page 198) and the fitted sheet (page 202), and fold the flat sheet through step 4 (page 200).

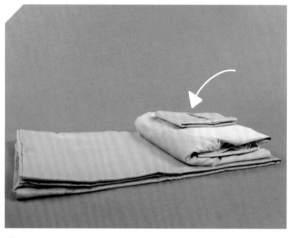

2 Place the folded pillowcase(s) on top of the folded fitted sheet, and then place these on the top half of the flat sheet.

3 Fold the flat sheet in half from bottom to top, with the folded pillowcase(s) and fitted sheet tucked inside. If the flat sheet has trim, make sure it is on top. Store on a shelf with the rounded edge facing out.

Janelle says...

Keeping sheet sets together is a great example of grab and go, making it easier for anyone in the household to make their beds.

Comforter

1 Lay the comforter horizontally on a flat surface. Fold in half from top to bottom, and then fold in half from right to left.

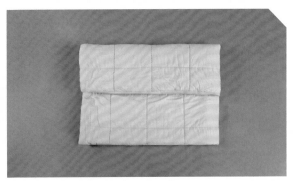

2 Bring down the top to the middle.

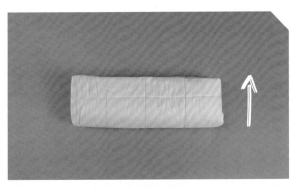

3 Fold up the bottom over the top.

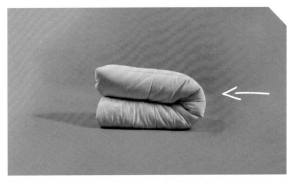

4 Fold in half from right to left.

5 If the comforter has trim, flip it over so that the trim is on top. Store on a shelf with the rounded edge facing out.

Janelle says...

Duvet covers can be folded using this same method.

Throw Blanket

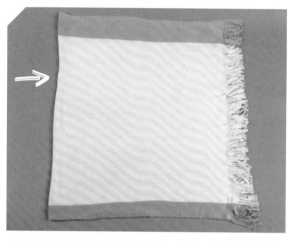

1 Lay the throw blanket horizontally on a flat surface. Fold in half from left to right.

2 Bring down the top to the middle.

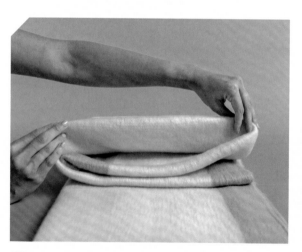

5 You have now created a pocket on the left side.

6 Tuck the right side of the blanket into the pocket.

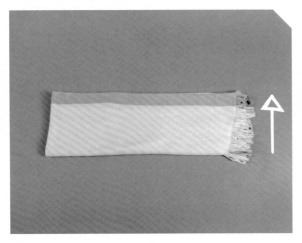

3 Fold up the bottom over the top.

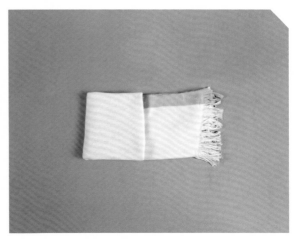

4 Fold in the left side to the middle.

7 Store on a shelf with the rounded edge facing out.

Dish Towel (Drawer)

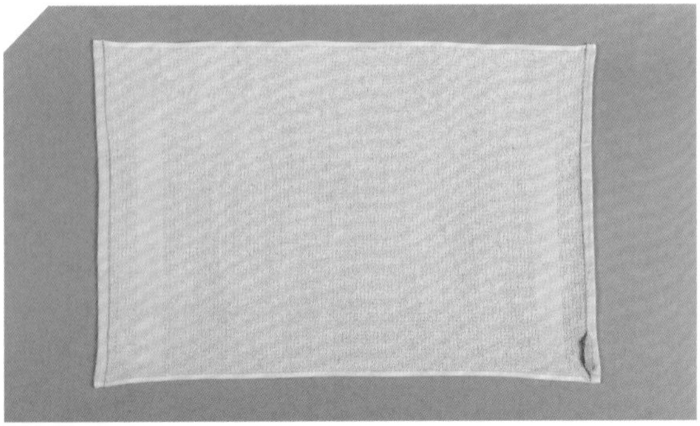

1 Lay the dish towel facedown horizontally on a flat surface.

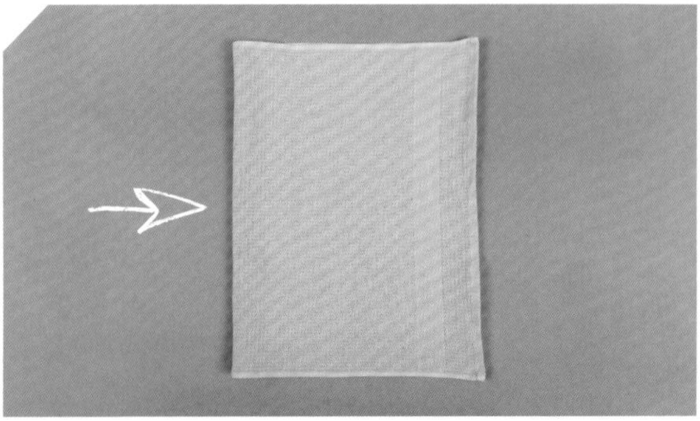

2 Fold in half from left to right.

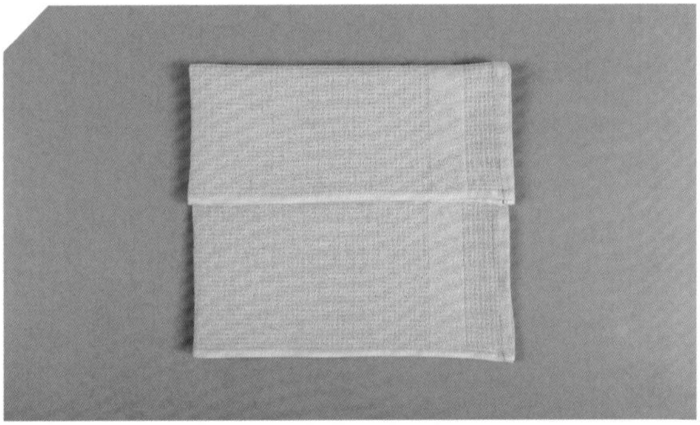

3 Bring down the top to the middle.

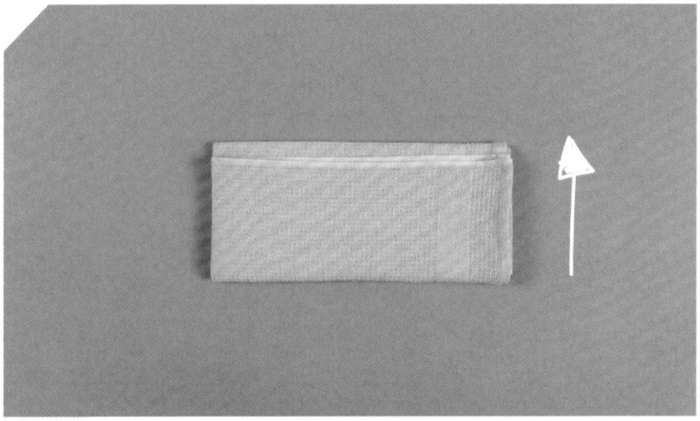

4 Fold up the bottom over the top.

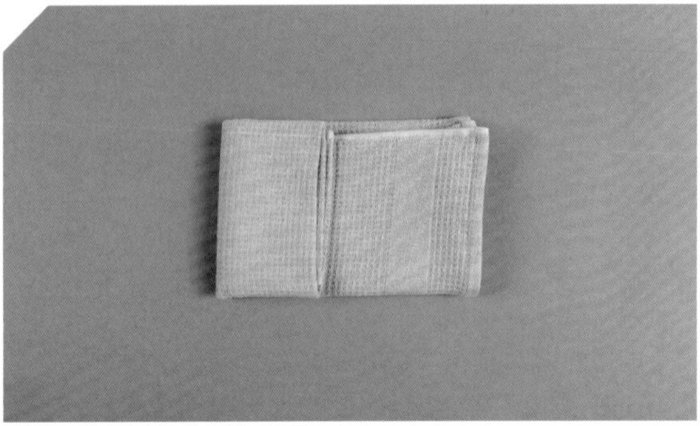

5 Fold in the left side to the middle.

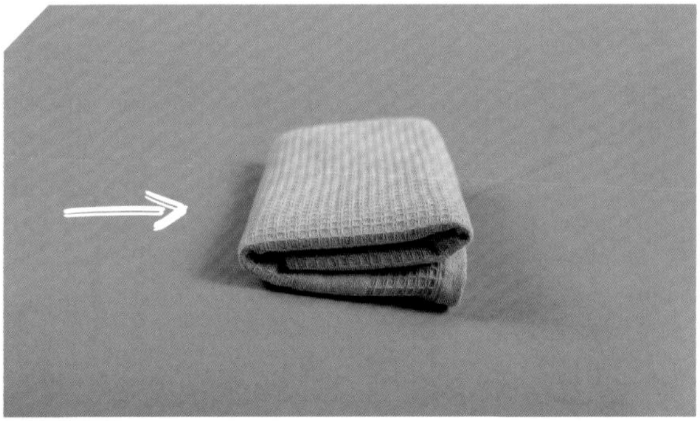

6 Fold the left side again and align with the right side. Place into a drawer with the rounded edge facing up.

Dish Towel (Hanging)

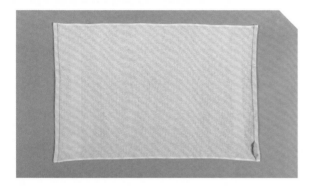

1 Lay the dish towel facedown horizontally on a flat surface.

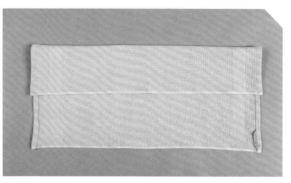

2 Bring down the top to the middle.

3 Fold up the bottom over the top.

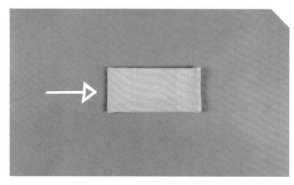

4 Fold in half from left to right.

5 Fold over a bar so that it is nice and even.

Janelle says...

If the dish towel has a graphic on it, the graphic side should be facedown in step 1.

211

Tablecloth (Rectangle)

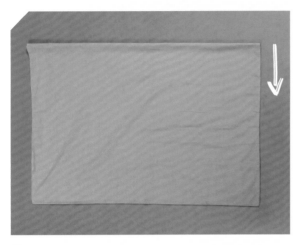

1 Lay the tablecloth horizontally on a flat surface. Fold in half from top to bottom.

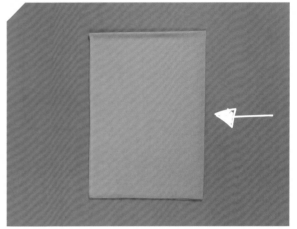

2 Fold in half again, from right to left.

3 Bring down the top to the middle.

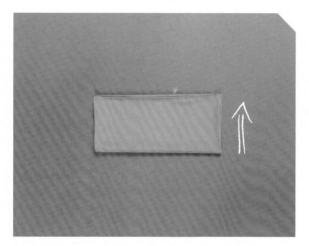

4 Fold up the bottom over the top.

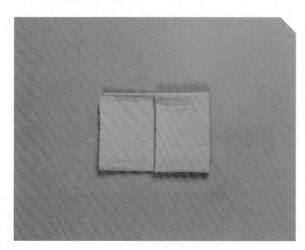

5 Fold in the right side to the middle.

6 Fold the left side over the right side. Store on a shelf with the rounded edge facing out.

Tablecloth (Round)

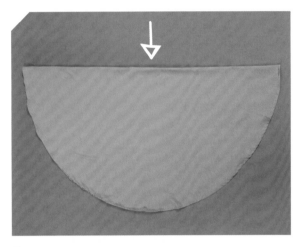

1 Lay the tablecloth on a flat surface. Fold in half from top to bottom to create a semicircle.

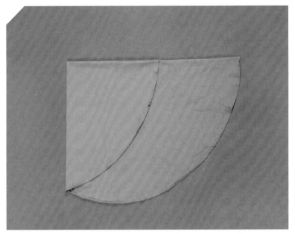

2 Fold in the left side to the middle.

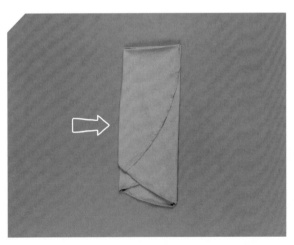

5 Take the piece you just folded over and fold it back to align with the right side.

6 Fold in half from bottom to top.

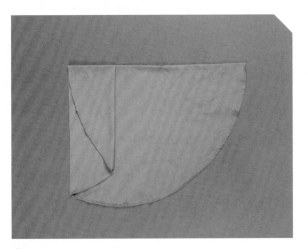

3 Take the piece you just folded over and fold it back to align with the left side.

4 Fold the right side over the left side, overcrossing it.

7 Flip over and store on a shelf with the rounded edge facing out.

Napkin

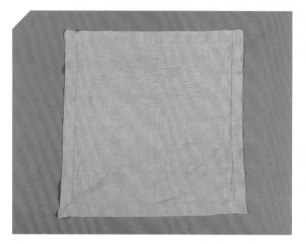

1 Lay the napkin facedown on a flat surface.

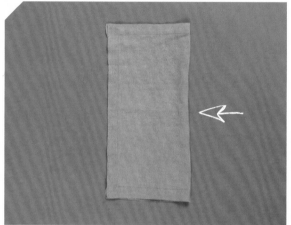

2 Fold in half from right to left.

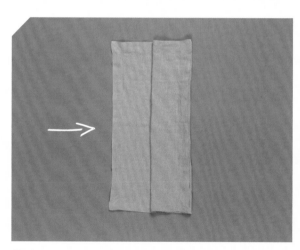

3 Take the piece you just folded and fold it back over itself.

Janelle says... Slide a menu into the pocket and tie a little ribbon or bow around the napkin for extra flair at your next dinner party!

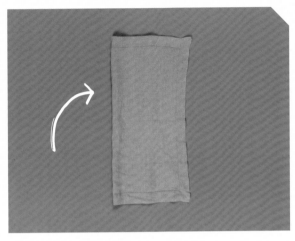

4 Flip the napkin over.

1
2

5 Bring up the bottom to the middle, and then fold the top over the bottom.

6 Flip it over so that the open flap is on the bottom. You can now slip silverware into the little pocket that was created.

Apron

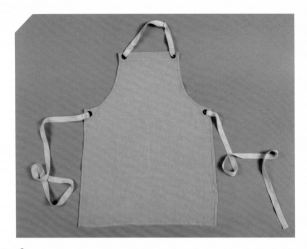

1 Lay the apron facedown on a flat surface.

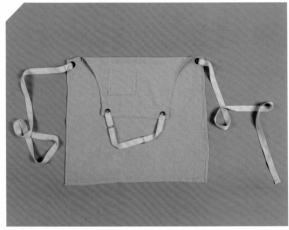

2 Fold down the top of the apron to create a straight line across the top. You want the apron to be a square shape.

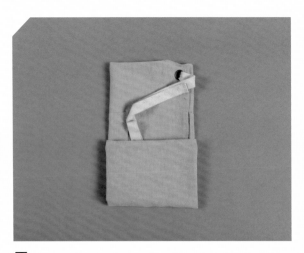

5 Bring up the bottom to the middle.

6 Fold up the bottom again and align with the top.

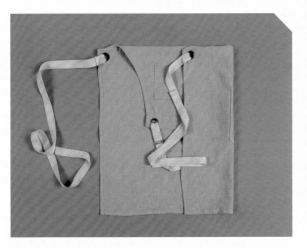

3 Fold in the right side to the middle, keeping the straps flat and smooth.

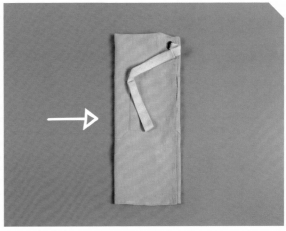

4 Fold the left side over the right side, adjusting the straps to keep them as flat as possible.

7 Place into a drawer with the rounded edge facing up.

Travel

Packing Tips
222

Packing Cubes
223

Dress
224

Jacket
226

Blazer
228

Cover-Up
230

Packing Tips

I really hate packing for a trip, and I know that most people feel the same way. It doesn't matter what I bring, when I get to my destination, I want to wear the opposite clothing of what I have packed. But what I will say is, I am a damn good packer. I may not know what to bring, but I can fill my suitcase and carry-on bag to their brims with an assortment of clothes and accessories because I know how to organize and fold everything well (and now so do you!). Though I cannot tell you what to pack (I wish I could!), here I share my tips for how to pack for travel.

Here are some tips to consider when packing:

1. **Comfort:** Now is not the time to pack something you never wear or a brand-new item you haven't tried on before.

2. **Weather:** There is nothing worse than not being prepared for the elements, especially if you're going to be outside at times.

3. **Activities:** Double-check your itinerary. You don't want to waste time having to shop for things you forgot to bring.

4. **Versatility:** Packing items that mix and match will allow for more outfit options.

5. **Multipurpose accessories:** Bring a bag and shoes for both daytime and nighttime that can be dressed up or down.

Packing Cubes

I have found packing cubes to be versatile and the best way to get the most space out of a suitcase, duffel, or backpack, especially when combined with the folding technique taught in this book. Packing cubes allow you to divide your items into categories and "Tetris" your travel bags effectively. If you Google "packing cubes," you will see that there are a lot of options out there in regard to number of bags in a set, fabrics, colors, patterns, and price points—basically something for everyone.

You may need to do a little online research to figure out what packing cubes are right for you.

Packing cubes can be packed a couple of different ways. I like to pack them by outfits or vibe (e.g., athleisure, fancy, pool), but other people prefer to pack them by clothing types (e.g., tops, bottoms, dresses). Neither one works better than the other; it just depends on what fits your needs.

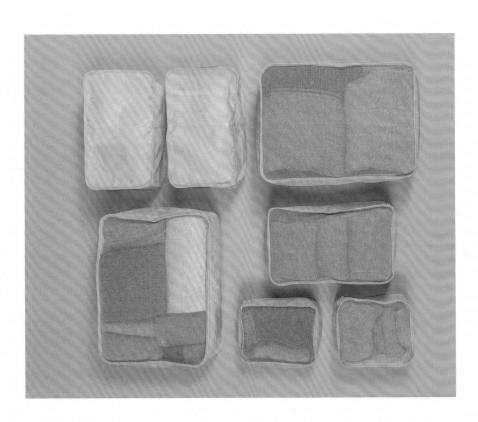

Dress

1 Lay the dress faceup on a flat surface.

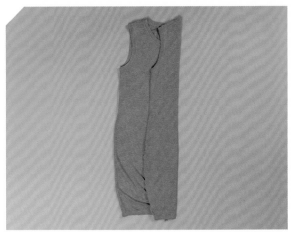

2 Fold in the right side to the middle.

5 Fold up the bottom one-quarter the length of the dress.

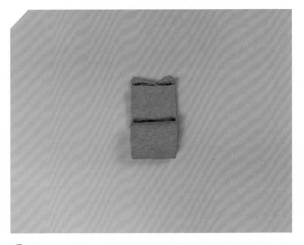

6 Continue folding up the bottom two more quarters.

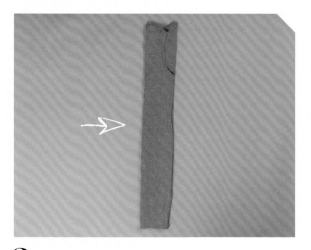

3 Fold in the left side over the right side.

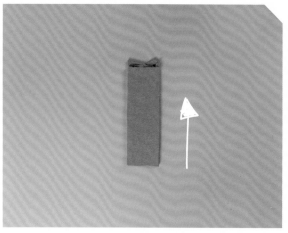

4 Bring up the bottom to right below the neckline.

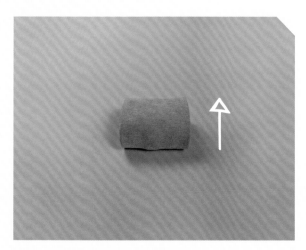

7 Fold up the final quarter and align with the top. Store in a packing cube with the rounded edge facing up. Immediately hang the dress once you reach your destination.

Janelle says . . .

In steps 5 and 6, this dress is folded into quarters, but the length of the dress will determine how many folds are needed. The longer the dress, the more folds you will need.

Jacket

1 Lay the jacket faceup on a flat surface. Zip or button the jacket to make it easier to fold.

2 Fold in half from right to left, making sure the sleeves are lined up.

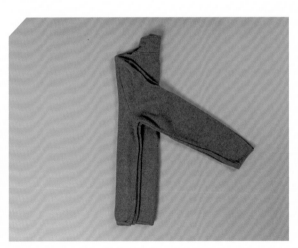

3 Fold the left side back halfway toward the right side.

> **Janelle says...** The thickness of the jacket will determine how many folds you need in step 6. The lighter the jacket the more folds you can make.

4 Fold the sleeves back and bend them down at the elbows so that they lie flat on the middle of the jacket.

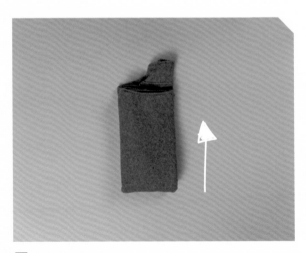

5 Bring up the bottom to right below the collar.

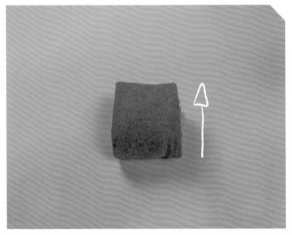

6 Fold in half from bottom to top. Place into a packing cube with the rounded edge facing up. Immediately hang the jacket once you reach your destination.

Blazer

1 Lay the blazer facedown on a flat surface. Button the jacket to make it easier to fold.

2 Fold in half from right to left, making sure the sleeves are lined up.

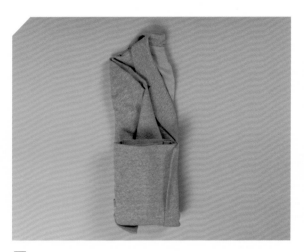

5 Fold up the bottom to the middle.

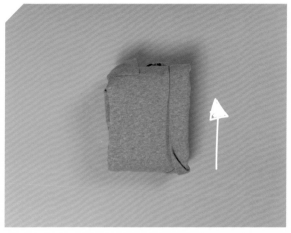

6 Fold up the bottom again and align with the top.

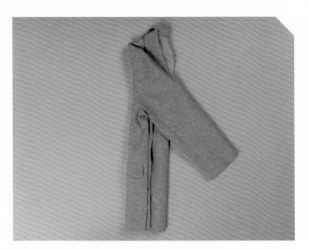

3 Fold the left side back halfway toward the right side.

4 Fold the sleeves back and bend them down at the elbows so that they lie flat on the middle of the jacket.

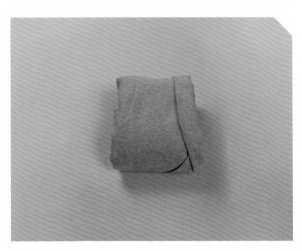

7 Place into a packing cube with the rounded edge facing up. Immediately hang the blazer once you reach your destination.

Cover-Up

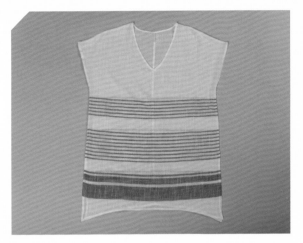

1 Lay the cover-up faceup on a flat surface.

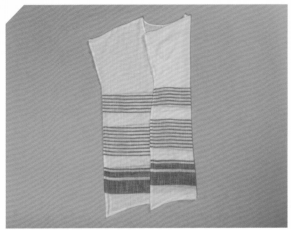

2 Fold in the right side to the middle.

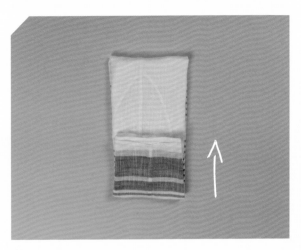

5 Fold up the bottom to the middle.

6 Bring up the bottom to the middle again.

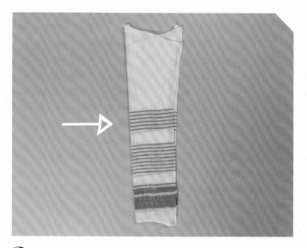

3 Fold in the left side over the right side.

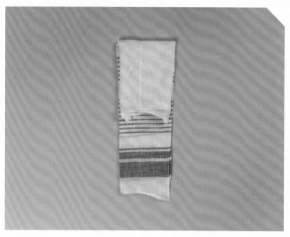

4 Bring down the top to the middle.

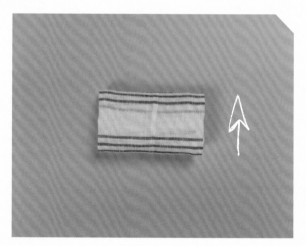

7 Fold up the bottom again and align with the top.

8 Place into a packing cube with the rounded edge facing up. Immediately hang the cover-up once you reach your destination.

Index

A

accessories
Ankle Socks (Basics), 45
Ankle Socks (Kid), 185
Bandana Bib, 138–139
Bib, 137
Beanie, 136
Calf Socks, 46–47
Burp Cloth, 142–143
No-Show Socks, 44
Sleep Sack, 146–147
Socks (Baby), 135
Tie, 92
adult
Ankle Socks, 45
Bike Shorts, 62–63
Bikini, 78–79
Bikini Underwear, 84–85
Blazer, 228–229
Bodysuit, 74–75
Boxer Briefs, 99
Boxers, 98
Bralette, 80
Calf Socks, 46–47
Cardigan, 32–33
Casual Pants/Denim, 38
Cover-Up, 230–231
Cropped Sweatshirt, 58–59
Cropped Tank Top, 50–51
Dress, 224–225
Dress Pants (Hanger), 39
Dress Pants (Shelf), 40–41
Flowy Tank Top, 52–53
Hoodie, 36–37
Jacket, 226–227

Leggings, 64–65
Long-Sleeve Button-Down, 28–29
Long-Sleeve T-Shirt, 26–27
Nightgown, 72–73
No-Show Socks, 44
One-Piece Swimsuit, 76–77
Padded Bra, 81
Pajama Bottoms, 96–97
Pajama Set, 69–71
Polo Shirt, 90–91
Shorts (Feminine), 60–61
Shorts (Masculine), 93
Short-Sleeve Button-Down, 25
Short-Sleeve Crop Top, 57
Short-Sleeve T-Shirt, 22–23
Short-Sleeve T-Shirt (Variation), 24
Skirt, 66–67
Skirt (Variation), 68
Sports Bra (Thick Straps), 82
Sports Bra (Thin Adjustable Straps), 83
Sweater, 30–31
Sweatpants, 42–43
Sweatshirt, 34–35
Swim Trunks, 94–95
Tank Top, 20–21
Thong, 86–87
Tie, 92
Tube Top, 56
Workout Tank Top, 54–55
ankle socks
Ankle Socks (Basics), 45
Ankle Socks (Kid), 185

Apron, 218–219
Athletic Shorts, 166–167

B

Baby
Bandana Bib, 138–139
Beanie, 136
Bib, 137
Bloomers, 116
Burp Cloth, 142–143
Crib Sheet, 148–151
Dress, 124–125
Hooded Towel, 140–141
Leggings, 120–121
Muslin Blanket, 144–145
One-Piece Swimsuit, 132–133
Overalls, 123
Pajamas, 110–111
Pants, 118–119
Shorts, 117
Short-Sleeve Onesie, 104–105
Short-Sleeve Romper, 108–109
Short-Sleeve T-Shirt, 112–113
Sleep Sack, 146–147
Sleeveless Onesie, 102–103
Sleeveless Romper, 106–107
Socks, 135
Sweat Suit, 126–128
Sweatpants, 122
Sweatshirt, 114–115
Swim Trunks, 134
Two-Piece Swimsuit, 129–131
Bandana Bib, 138–139
Basics
Ankle Socks, 45

Calf Socks, 46–47
Cardigan, 32–33
Casual Pants/Denim, 38
Dress Pants (Hanger), 39
Dress Pants (Shelf), 40–41
Hoodie, 36–37
Long-Sleeve Button-Down,
   28–29
Long-Sleeve T-Shirt, 26–27
No-Show Socks, 44
Short-Sleeve Button-Down, 25
Short-Sleeve T-Shirt, 22–23
Short-Sleeve T-Shirt
   (Variation), 24
Sweater, 30–31
Sweatpants, 42–43
Sweatshirt, 34–35
Tank Top, 20–21
Bath Towel, 194–195
bathing suits. See swimsuits.
bathroom
   Bath Towel, 194–195
   Hand Towel, 193
   Washcloth, 192
Beanie, 136
bedding
   Comforter, 207
   Crib Sheet, 148–151
   Fitted Sheet, 202–205
   Flat Sheet, 200–201
   Pillowcase, 198–199
   Sheet Set, 206
   Throw Blanket, 208–209
bibs
   Bib, 137
   Bandana Bib, 138–139
Bike Shorts, 62–63
Bikini, 78–79

Bikini Underwear, 84–85
blankets
   Comforter, 207
   Muslin Blanket, 144–145
   Throw Blanket, 208–209
Blazer, 228–229
Bloomers, 116
Bodysuit, 74–75
booty point, definition of, 16
boxer briefs
   Boxer Briefs (Kid), 188–189
   Boxer Briefs (Masculine), 99
Boxers, 98
bras
   Bralette, 80
   Padded Bra, 81
   Sports Bra (Thick Straps), 82
   Sports Bra (Thin Adjustable
      Straps), 83
Burp Cloth, 142–143
button-downs
   Long-Sleeve Button-Down,
      28–29
   Short-Sleeve Button-Down
      (Basics), 25
   Short-Sleeve Button-Down
      (Kid), 158

C
Calf Socks, 46–47
cardigans
   Cardigan (Basics), 32–33
   Cardigan (Kid), 162–163
Casual Pants/Denim, 38
Comforter, 207
Cover-Up, 230–231
Crib Sheet, 148–151
crop tops

Cropped Sweatshirt, 58–59
Cropped Tank Top, 50–51
Short-Sleeve Crop Top, 57
Cubes, Packing, 223

D
denim. See Casual Pants/Denim.
dish towels
   Dish Towel (Drawer), 210
   Dish Towel (Hanging), 211
dresses
   Dress (Baby), 124–125
   Dress (Kid), 170–171
   Dress (Travel), 224–225
dress pants
   Dress Pants (Hanger), 39
   Dress Pants (Shelf), 40–41

F
facedown, definition of, 16
faceup, definition of, 16
Feminine
   Bike Shorts, 62–63
   Bikini, 78–79
   Bikini Underwear, 84–85
   Bodysuit, 74–75
   Bralette, 80
   Cropped Sweatshirt, 58–59
   Cropped Tank Top, 50–51
   Flowy Tank Top, 52–53
   Leggings, 64–65
   Nightgown, 72–73
   One-Piece Swimsuit, 76–77
   Padded Bra, 81
   Pajama Set, 69–71
   Shorts, 60–61
   Short-Sleeve Crop Top, 57
   Skirt, 66–67

Skirt (Variation), 68
Sports Bra (Thick Straps), 82
Sports Bra (Thin Adjustable
    Straps), 83
Thong, 86–87
Tube Top, 56
Workout Tank Top, 54–55
file folding, 12–13
Fitted Sheet, 202–205
Flat Sheet, 200–201
Flowy Tank Top, 52–53
fold in half, definition of, 16
fold in thirds, definition of, 16
folding
    basics, 14
    editing while, 15
    labeling a kid's dresser, 11
    organizing dressers, 11
    technique, 12–13
    vs. hanging, 10

G
grab and go, definition of, 16

H
Hand Towel, 193
Hooded Towel, 140–141
hoodies
    Hoodie (Basics), 36–37
    Hoodie (Kid), 164–165

J
Jacket, 226–227
jeans. *See* Casual Pants/Denim.

K
Kid
    Ankle Socks, 185

Athletic Shorts, 166–167
Boxer Briefs, 188–189
Cardigan, 162–163
Dress, 170–171
Hoodie, 164–165
Long-Sleeve T-Shirt, 160–161
One-Piece Swimsuit, 180–181
Pajama Set, 177–179
Pants, 169
Polo Shirt, 159
Shorts, 168
Short-Sleeve Button-Down, 158
Short-Sleeve T-Shirt
    (Variation), 157
Short-Sleeve T-Shirt, 156
Skirt, 172–173
Sweat Suit, 174–176
Swim Trunks, 184
Tank Top, 154–155
Two-Piece Swimsuit, 182–183
Underwear, 186–187
kitchen
    Apron, 218–219
    Dish Towel (Drawer), 210
    Dish Towel (Hanging), 211
    Napkin, 216–217
    Tablecloth (Rectangle),
        212–213
    Tablecloth (Round),
        214–215

L
Leggings
    Leggings (Baby), 120–121
    Leggings (Feminine), 64–65
legs, definition of, 16
Linens
    Apron, 218–219

Bath Towel, 194–195
Comforter, 207
Dish Towel (Drawer), 210
Dish Towel (Hanging), 211
Fitted Sheet, 202–205
Flat Sheet, 200–201
Hand Towel, 193
Napkin, 216–217
Pillowcase, 198–199
Robe, 196–197
Sheet Set, 206
Tablecloth (Rectangle), 212–213
Tablecloth (Round), 214–215
Throw Blanket, 208–209
Washcloth, 192
Long-Sleeve Button-Down,
    28–29
long-sleeve T-shirts
    Long-Sleeve T-Shirt
        (Basics), 26–27
    Long-Sleeve T-Shirt
        (Kid), 160–161

M
Masculine
    Boxer Briefs, 99
    Boxers, 98
    Pajama Bottoms, 96–97
    Polo Shirt, 90–91
    Shorts, 93
    Swim Trunks, 94–95
    Tie, 92
Muslin Blanket, 144–145

N
Napkin, 216–217
Nightgown, 72–73
No-Show Socks, 44

O

one-piece swimsuits
    One-Piece Swimsuit (Baby),
       132–133
    One-Piece Swimsuit
       (Feminine), 76–77
    One-Piece Swimsuit (Kid),
       180–181
onesies
    Short-Sleeve Onesie,
       104–105
    Sleeveless Onesie, 102–103
Overalls, 123
overcrossing, definition of, 16

P

packing
    Packing Cubes, 223
    Packing Tips, 222
Padded Bra, 81
Pajama Bottoms, 96–97
pajama sets
    Pajama Set (Feminine), 69–71
    Pajama Set (Kid), 177–179
Pajamas, 110–111
pants
    Casual Pants/Denim, 38
    Dress Pants (Hanger), 39
    Dress Pants (Shelf), 40–41
    Leggings (Baby), 120–121
    Leggings (Feminine), 64–65
    Pajama Bottoms, 96–97
    Pants (Baby), 118–119
    Pants (Kid), 169
    Sweatpants (Baby), 122
    Sweatpants (Basics), 42–43
Pillowcase, 198–199
polo shirts

Polo Shirt (Kid), 159
Polo Shirt (Masculine), 90–91

R

Robe, 196–197
rompers
    Short-Sleeve Romper, 108–109
    Sleeveless Romper, 106–107
rounded edge, definition of, 16

S

sheets
    Crib Sheet, 148–151
    Fitted Sheet, 202–205
    Flat Sheet, 200–201
    Sheet Set, 206
short-sleeve button-downs
    Short-Sleeve Button-Down
       (Basics), 25
    Short-Sleeve Button-Down (Kid),
       158
Short-Sleeve Crop Top, 57
Short-Sleeve Onesie, 104–105
Short-Sleeve Romper, 108–109
short-sleeve T-shirts
    Short-Sleeve T-Shirt (Baby),
       112–113
    Short-Sleeve T-Shirt (Basics),
       22–23
    Short-Sleeve T-Shirt (Kid), 156
    Short-Sleeve T-Shirt Variation
       (Basics), 24
    Short-Sleeve T-Shirt Variation
       (Kid), 157
shorts
    Athletic Shorts, 166–167
    Bike Shorts, 62–63
    Bloomers, 116

Shorts (Baby), 117
Shorts (Feminine), 60–61
Shorts (Kid), 168
Shorts (Masculine), 93
skirts
    Skirt (Feminine), 66–67
    Skirt (Kid), 172–173
    Skirt Variation (Feminine), 68
Sleep Sack, 146–147
Sleeveless Onesie, 102–103
Sleeveless Romper, 106–107
socks
    Ankle Socks (Basics), 45
    Ankle Socks (Kid), 185
    Calf Socks, 46–47
    No-Show Socks, 44
    Socks (Baby), 135
sports bras
    Sports Bra (Thick Straps), 82
    Sports Bra (Thin Adjustable
       Straps), 83
Straighten Up by Janelle, 8
Sweater, 30–31
sweats
    Cropped Sweatshirt, 58–59
    Hoodie (Basics), 36–37
    Hoodie (Kid), 164–165
    Sweat Suit (Baby), 126–128
    Sweat Suit (Kid), 174–176
    Sweatpants (Baby), 122
    Sweatpants (Basics), 42–43
    Sweatshirt (Baby), 114–115
    Sweatshirt (Basics), 34–35
swim trunks
    Swim Trunks (Baby), 134
    Swim Trunks (Kid), 184
    Swim Trunks (Masculine),
       94–95

swimsuits
  Bikini, 78–79
  One-Piece Swimsuit (Baby),
    132–133
  One-Piece Swimsuit (Feminine),
    76–77
  One-Piece Swimsuit (Kid),
    180–181
  Swim Trunks (Baby), 134
  Swim Trunks (Kid), 184
  Swim Trunks (Masculine), 94–95
  Two-Piece Swimsuit (Baby),
    129–131
  Two-Piece Swimsuit (Baby),
    129–131
  Two-Piece Swimsuit (Kid),
    182–183

T

T-shirts
  Long-Sleeve T-Shirt (Basics),
    26–27
  Long-Sleeve T-Shirt (Kid),
    160–161
  Short-Sleeve Crop Top, 57
  Short-Sleeve T-Shirt (Baby),
    112–113
  Short-Sleeve T-Shirt (Basics),
    22–23
  Short-Sleeve T-Shirt (Kid), 156
  Short-Sleeve T-Shirt Variation
    (Basics), 24
  Short-Sleeve T-Shirt Variation
    (Kid), 157
tablecloths
  Tablecloth (Rectangle),
    212–213
  Tablecloth (Round), 214–215

tank tops
  Cropped Tank Top, 50–51
  Flowy Tank Top, 52–53
  Tank Top (Basics), 20–21
  Tank Top (Kid), 154–155
  Workout Tank Top, 54–55
towels
  Bath Towel, 194–195
  Dish Towel (Drawer), 210
  Dish Towel (Hanging), 211
  Hand Towel, 193
  Hooded Towel, 140–141
Thong, 86–87
Throw Blanket, 208–209
Tie, 92
Travel
  Blazer, 228–229
  Cover-Up, 230–231
  Dress, 224–225
  Jacket, 226–227
  Packing Cubes, 223
  Packing Tips, 222
Tube Top, 56
two-piece swimsuits
  Bikini, 78–79
  Two-Piece Swimsuit (Baby),
    129–131
  Two-Piece Swimsuit (Kid),
    182–183

U

underwear
  Bikini Underwear, 84–85
  Boxer Briefs (Kid), 188–189
  Boxer Briefs (Masculine), 99
  Boxers, 98
  Thong, 86–87
  Underwear (Kid), 186–187

W

Washcloth, 192
workout clothes
  Bike Shorts, 62–63
  Leggings, 64–65
  Sports Bra (Thick Straps), 82
  Sports Bra (Thin Adjustable
    Straps), 83
  Workout Tank Top, 54–55

**Clothing sizes featured
throughout this book:**

Basics: medium
Feminine: medium
Masculine: large
Baby: 6–9 months
Kid: 4T

Acknowledgments

I never in my wildest dreams thought that I would be lucky enough to have the opportunity to write a book. It has not only been the hardest and most rewarding accomplishment I have ever achieved, but it has also been life-changing.

There are so many people to thank, first and foremost my incredible mom, dad, and sister, Danielle.

To my mom, Lainie. You are the ultimate mother. You have truly led by example in how to be a strong woman who can do it all. I hope to be half the mother you are to me. You have guided me through this whole process by supporting me and reminding me that I have the power within me to do anything I set my mind to. (And thank you for steaming/ironing a million pieces of clothing on set!)

To my dad, Steve, the OG entrepreneur. You have shown me what it means to be innovative, to always be learning, and to do everything at 200 percent. Whenever I need your advice, you are always there to share your wisdom and help me see things from a different perspective. Thank you for all you did to help make this book come to life. I could not have done it without you.

To my incredible little sister, Danielle, my best friend and partner in crime. The best day of my life was the day you were born, and I am so grateful to have you by my side through everything. You have helped me grow my business, been my biggest supporter through every win, and propped me up through every curveball. Everyone should be lucky enough to have a sister like you.

To Mary Claire Roman, my fabulous photographer and friend. When I started writing this book, I knew the photography would be a huge undertaking. I immediately called you knowing that you could make my vision for this book come to life. Thank you for the millions of hours dancing together in the studio, patiently waiting for me to make each and every fold perfect, and being so dang talented.

None of this would have been possible without my amazing friends, who truly stepped up and helped in so many different ways.

To Sophie Levine, my ride or die. I literally couldn't survive without you. You have been by my side through it all and our shared laughter makes every day better. Thank you for being my sister and chosen family.

To Mia Marcon, the definition of what it means to be a friend. You amaze me in everything you do. You remember all the small things, and your love is truly unconditional.

To Isa Briones, who came to every photo shoot and made sure I was always smiling, looking good, and having fun. You are a true angel who always goes above and beyond.

To Steve Levine, a legend who has guided me in life in so many ways. Thank you for reminding me that all the best things come from jumping off the edge. I love you endlessly.

To the strong women, who are no longer here with me but are deep in my heart, Linda Levine, Sheri Goldner, Grandma Sylvia, and Chana Schachner. I know you all would have supported me in any way I needed. From my style to my sass, you have all gifted a little piece of yourselves that have made me who I am.

To Ed, Liane, Everett, and Spencer. Thank you for welcoming me into your family all those years ago and letting me write my book at your house. You all hold such a special place in my heart, and I am lucky to have you.

To the rest of my family (hey, aunts, uncles, and cousins!) and extended family (Bruckner family et al.—you know who you are). Thank you for being my cheerleaders through it all. A special shout out to Allison Langus, who is family I am lucky enough to call a best friend; Ali Bruckner, who has helped me transform my business and life; Chance Taylor, who is like my brother and life is better with you in it; and my UCLA crew, who are the best friends a girl could ask for.

To my agent, Andrianna Yeatts at ICM. Thank you for guiding me through this whole process and taking care of me in so many ways. You went above the call of duty, and I am so grateful.

To Ali Berman. I can never express what you mean to me. You have truly shown me what it means to be a boss. You have helped me and guided me without expecting anything in return, and I hope that I can pass your kindness forward to other women.

To the incredible team at Quarto, especially Rage, Erin, and Laura. You made my dream become a reality, and you did so with such care and perfection. Thank you for the endless calls, emails, edits, and brainstorming. This would have never happened without your innovation and hard work.

A huge shout out to all my assistants, especially Chet Norment. You help me get everything done each day. I could absolutely never do any of it without you. Thank you for sticking by my side, saying yes to all my crazy ideas, and taking necessary dance breaks mid-project. This business thrives because of you.

To my amazing hair stylist, Ashley Marer, and makeup artist, Christina Adams. Thank you for making me feel like my best self for the photo shoots and being incredible women.

To the Farber family. Thank you for letting me take over your house for my photo shoots and supporting me in so many ways. You all went out of your way to help me, and I will forever be grateful.

To Jay Shetty and Radhi Devlukia. Thank you for all your support and opening up your home to my crew in the middle of moving day to shoot at your house. I am so appreciative.

To all my incredible clients, who have allowed me to make a career for myself doing what I love. Every project, every person, and every referral are so special to me, and I wake up every day ecstatic that I am able to live my dreams. Welcoming me into your homes and lives is a huge gesture that I am forever grateful for.

Thank you to everyone who has purchased this book, read it, and used it to better their lives. It is amazing to get to share what I love with all of you.

And last but certainly not least, to my little Levi, who cracked open my heart months ago. You bring me joy and unconditional love every day.

About the Author

Janelle Cohen empowers people from all walks of life to regain control over their spaces and, by extension, their lives. A professional organizer, interior decorator, and entrepreneur, she has taken her personal passions and turned them into a thriving business that allows her to help others where—and when—they need it most. Her clients include household names such as Jordyn Woods (with whom her work was featured on *MTV Cribs*), Emma Chamberlain, Jay Shetty, and more, many of them everyday families looking to bring the magic back into their day-to-day lives. Janelle has also been featured in numerous publications and websites, including *People, Star Magazine, House Beautiful*, and Apartment Therapy, and has brought unique yet accessible content to even more audiences through her partnerships with beloved brands such as BuzzFeed, Headspace, and The Container Store.

Janelle builds personal and intimate relationships with her clients, treating their spaces and their dreams for them as sacred. Most are long-term, recurring relationships, and she's proud to be a part of each milestone for those whom she works with as they progress through the years. Despite this, her goal is ultimately not only to help but also to teach, creating sustainable solutions that others can maintain and replicate on their own. She hopes to place the skills and tools she has developed over the years into the hands of countless others by codifying knowledge that is seldom taught but often sorely needed. In doing so, she continues to inspire individuals and families around the globe to take charge of their past, present, and future, starting with their own homes.